you ask about . . .

LiFE

Questions Teens are asking

by Tim **Pauls**

CONCORDIA PUBLISHING HOUSE · SAINT LOUIS

Copyright © 2006
Concordia Publishing House
3558 S. Jefferson Avenue,
St. Louis, MO 63118-3968
www.cph.org 1-800-325-3040

Library of Congress Cataloging-in-Publication Data
Pauls, Tim, 1967 —
  You ask about life: questions teens are asking / by Tim Pauls.
    p. cm.
ISBN 0-7586-1006-8
1. Lutheran youth — Religious life — Miscellanea. 2. Theology, Doctrinal — Miscellanea.
3. Lutheran Church — Missouri Synod — Doctrines—Miscellanea. I. Title.
Bx8074.Y68P38 2006
230'.41—dc22   20005038043

1 2 3 4 5 6 7 8 9 10   15 14 13 12 11 10 09 08 07 06

For Nathan, whose avid
interest in life and pursuit
of answers makes my day.
Thanks, as always, to Pastor
Mike McCoy, fellow pastor,
writer, doctrine-checker, and
one who has taught me much
about proclaiming the truth
of Jesus in a dying world.

Table of Contents

8 Why Should You Spend Part of Your Life Reading this Book?

Questions, questions. There are tons of questions out there, and you probably get them all the time. I know I do: "What about evolution?" "Can soldiers be Christians?" "Should there be prayer in public schools?" "Between your fascinating sermons and your devastating handsomeness, how do you manage to stay so modest?" Yup, I get them all the time . . . well, most of those, anyway.

There's an infinite number of questions out there, and there are even more answers—the problem is that most of the answers are wrong. People come up with different answers for a couple of different reasons. For one, some people believe that there's no such thing as truth. Therefore, whatever you believe is true, because you believe it. In fact, I've even heard some individuals say that 2+2=5 isn't wrong, as long as you can give a good reason for the answer. Wow! I can hardly wait until those guys start building airplanes, skyscrapers, bridges, and things. As for me, I'll stick with the idea that there is such a thing as truth and error; right and wrong.

Other people come up with different answers because they have different sources of information. They rely on their gut feelings to tell them what's what. They follow the teachings of a certain person, philosophy, or religion. These days, a lot of people seem to get their answers from a couple of really scary sources—the loudest talker or public opinion. It seems that whatever a lot of other people say must be true, because they're saying it. However, you know full well that loud people aren't necessarily right, just noisy; and crowds have been wrong before.

None of this is good enough for you. When you ask questions about life, it's because the answers you find affect your life for the rest of your life. Sometimes, your life may quite literally depend on

9

the answers. With questions like these, you want to be certain that the answers are correct.

This book contains a bunch of questions and answers. It has its limits—there are a lot of questions that don't get answered here. But here's the best reason to read this book—the answers are true. They are true because they follow God's Word and it's the final authority. What's more, the questions and answers in this book are designed to help you find answers to questions that aren't in this book.

So here's the plan for the pages that follow:

✱ I'm a pastor, so I'm going to answer questions like a pastor. I'm not an engineer, a scientist, a psychologist, or a professional football player, so I'm not going to answer like they would. You'll see what I mean later on.

✱ Even though I'm going to answer as a pastor, that doesn't mean that the answers will only come from the Bible. When dealing with daily life, God sometimes gives us answers to questions through things like science and even a rare commodity called common sense. From time to time we'll also mention God's gift called the conscience. These are excellent sources for answers, so we can use them as long as we don't use them to contradict Scripture.

✱ If I'm guessing, I promise to tell you. The Bible does not directly answer every question that pops up in life. Sometimes that means we need to give an answer based on some general truth from

Scripture. Sometimes it means that the Bible simply leaves the decision up to you. But if the answer is just me giving my own personal opinion, I'll let you know. The Lord requires you to trust and obey His Word—He says nothing about binding you to my views.

* Along with that, keep in mind that life is messy. God's Word is black and white, but life in a sinful world is full of grays. Sometimes Christians expect that every decision they face will have a clear right and wrong. I wish this were true, but it isn't. You'll especially see this when we discuss things like prayer in public schools or end of life issues.

* I should probably say something about what you won't find in this book. People have a lot of questions about relationships—dating, boyfriends, sex, family, and more. You won't find those questions in this book, because there are so many. You will find them in a sequel to this book called *You Ask about Relationships: Questions Teens Are Asking.*

In looking at the subject matter, I realize that a lot of these issues weren't discussed among my peers when I was a teenager. But then I can think of a lot of youth today who are asking these questions. Times have certainly changed, and not especially for the better. You've got a lot more junk to deal with in this world than I did when I was in high school, and that really wasn't all that long ago.

So there you go. That's why you should read this book. It's a book of true answers based upon God's

Word that show you what we know, what we don't know, what's right, what's certain, and what we can't be sure of. Underlying all of this, however, is a glorious, certain truth—even though life is full of tough questions, hard answers, and some unexplainable messes, you can be absolutely sure that you're a child of God for the sake of Jesus. You're not going to answer every question well in life and get a perfect score; thanks be to God that your salvation doesn't depend on that. Instead, your salvation is already won in Jesus who died on the cross and rose again to redeem you from sin to everlasting life.

Unlike so many answers in this world, that saying is sure.

Read on, and the Lord be with you!

Pastor Tim Pauls

Section One: Witnesses

> Warning! if you skip this section, puppies will no longer like you and you may contract scurvy, rickets, or one of those other hideous diseases that you read about in history books.

Not really, but I'm trying to make sure that you read this section. If you read books like I read books, you want to skip the dry, boring introductory stuff and get right to the exciting parts. The following may look terribly dry, boring and introductory—but it's not. It's the most important part. Without this part, the rest of the book won't make nearly as much sense. Besides, it includes a drawn-out analogy about a goldfish named Mr. Sloopy, and how could you not read about that?

You've probably seen a few courtroom scenes on television or in the movies. Courtrooms are all about proving the truth with evidence. The prosecutor puts witnesses on the stand to testify, to tell the truth about what they've seen or heard. But before he does so, he wants to make sure that the witnesses are trustworthy. He wants to find out what they know and what they don't know. He wants to make certain how they can help and how they can't.

If we're going to ask and answer all sorts of questions about life, we need witnesses to tell us about life. Before we listen to the witnesses, we need to know what they know and how they can help. We need to know how they get along, what their limitations are, and where their answers might be misused or misunderstood. That's the purpose of this first section, and it's the most important part of this book. Why? As the old Chinese proverb says, "Give a man a fish and he eats for a day; teach a man to fish and he eats for a lifetime." This is a very helpful proverb. It is almost as valuable for life as this one: "If a Pauls goes fishing to catch dinner for you, you'd better know how to order pizza."

My point is this: I could just give you a bunch of answers to a bunch of questions, and you'd know a bunch of stuff. But while knowing stuff is good, it's much better if you know how to think. If you know how to think, then you can answer more questions on your own without having to ask someone else or hoping the answer pops up in a book like this.

So this is my super-secret hidden agenda in this book—every question and answer isn't just designed to *give* you information, but to help you *think* through issues. But this is a covert ploy, so make sure you don't tell yourself. We'll keep this just between you and me.

The Purpose of the Witnesses—Truth

Back to the witnesses. To answer questions about life, we'll be using four important witnesses:

Scripture

Science

Common sense

Conscience

Each one of these is a gift from God. Often, people try to make them look like they contradict each other, but they don't. Once you understand their purposes and limitations, they get along quite well.

s c r i p t u r e

Though He used men to write it down, the Bible *is* God's Word. The purpose of God's Word is to tell you about God's plan of salvation for you. Because the Bible is God's Word, it is without error and completely trustworthy. The Bible is the final authority of right and wrong, and it's *the* source of information about Jesus Christ, God's only-begotten Son who died on the cross to take away your sins.

science

Science is the study of the creation, the process of discovering the truth about nature. The purpose of science includes discovering truth about the world around you. For something to be true in science, it must be proven. To prove something, people use the scientific method. The scientific method includes four steps:

1. You see something.

2. You guess what happened.

3. You test your guess.

4. You repeat your test, several times, to make sure it wasn't some sort of freaky result the first time.

When something happens again and again, then it's a scientific truth.

For instance, let's say you have a fishbowl in your room. You see that your goldfish, which for some unknown reason you've named Mr. Sloopy, is barely swimming and staring at nothing with his disturbingly bulbous eyes. You guess that Mr. Sloopy is hungry.

17

You test your guess by giving him some food; and sure enough, he's now swimming around the tank quite happily and staring at you with those disturbingly bulbous eyes.

The following day, you notice that Mr. Sloopy is listless again, so you repeat your test by feeding him, and he's back to doing all those fun goldfish things. This cycle proves to be true day after day. You thus conclude that goldfish need food in order to live happy and productive lives . . . whatever that may mean in goldfish terms. You have established a truth scientifically.

Whether you know it or not, you have been trained to think scientifically. This is a good thing. When it comes to dealing with the things of this world, you want proof before you believe something. If you have hay fever, you don't take Mr. Sloopy's deworming medicine and hope it will help—you take the medicine scientifically proven to treat your allergy.

That's how science works, whether dealing with archeology, astronomy, biology, psychology, microwaving toast, or skateboarding. People discover truth by observing, guessing, testing, and repeating.

Science is not your enemy. I love science. It's a gift from God—properly used, science remains a great blessing.

common sense

God has given you the ability to think, reason, and use common sense. You are able to think for yourself, to ask questions and not believe everything you hear.

You can often figure out the truth without other people telling you, because sometimes "things just make sense." That's the purpose of common sense, to enable you to make logical conclusions about what is true in the world. Common sense is really a cousin of science—when you figured out the need to feed your goldfish, you used common sense to make a scientific conclusion. You didn't try mixing Jell-O™ into the water to help Mr. Sloopy, because you knew better. Common sense prevents you from getting hurt, getting used, or going in the wrong direction. Common sense requires practice and discipline to use. It's much easier to accept what other people say than to think through things yourself.

c o n s c i e n c e

Your conscience is also a gift from God, although you may not appreciate it. Most often the only time you become aware of your conscience is when it's troubling you because you've done something bad. Your conscience does this because God has written His Law on your heart (Romans 2:15); thus, your conscience also serves as a witness to what is true and right.

The Limitations
of Witnesses

If you're going to use these witnesses properly, you need to understand their limitations as well as their purpose.

19

scripture

Scripture was not given by God to be a science book. Don't misunderstand—the accounts in the Bible really happened in this world—and the Bible is accurate in its account. However, the purpose of Scripture is not to explain scientific truth. In other words, let's say that you want to be a rocket scientist, so you go to college and sign up for "Rocket Science 101." While all of your fellow geniuses go to the bookstore and buy lots and lots of books that make this one look reeeallly exciting, you say, "I'm not going to buy those books, I have my Bible, and that's all I need."

I don't want to ruin your day, champ, but you're not going to pass the class. God gives the Bible to tell you about salvation, while He provided a whole bunch of guys with names like Werner von Braun to write books about how to fly to the moon.

It seems pretty obvious, doesn't it? However, this happens a lot. For instance, recently someone published diet books that try to teach proper eating habits by looking at laws concerning foods in the Bible. But the Bible wasn't written as a guide to nutrition and fitness; it was written to tell you about Jesus Christ. You don't have to eat locusts to have a healthy diet! That comforting news should be worth the price of this book alone.

science

The following limitation is one of the most important parts in this book—in the world of science something is only considered true when it can be proven true scientifically. Likewise, in the world of science, something is only false when it can be proven false scientifically. An honest scientist will never say, "We can't prove it, so it must be wrong." Nor will he ever say, "We can't prove it, but it must be right." If science cannot prove something, then an honest scientist will say, "We don't know one way or the other." It remains an open question. It's a phenomenon, an unexplained mystery. But scientifically, it's neither true nor false.

For instance, your best friend comes to school and tells you that a fishbowl-shaped UFO landed in his backyard last night. A gurgling voice from inside the craft wanted to know how to find the Chosen Exalted Goldfish, Leader of the Universe, whom it called Mystrslu Pe. Now, did this really happen? Scientifically, you can't say yes or no. Aside from your friend, no one saw this. Unless the event repeats itself, it can't be tested. Therefore, honestly according to science, you can't say with absolute certainty that it did or didn't happen.

Common sense will tell you that it probably didn't, but there's still a remote possibility.

Common sense will also tell you that maybe you need a new best friend.

And maybe you'd better take better care of your goldfish, just in case.

At any rate, science can only prove those events

21

that it can observe and test. If it can't observe or test an event, it doesn't mean that it's right or wrong. It simply means that this event lies outside the realm of science. This will be very important when we get to questions like evolution or the miracles of Jesus, because people keep trying to say that science and the Bible disagree. They really don't, and here's why.

The Conflict That Almost Everybody Thinks Is True, But Truly Isn't

Because you've decided to take better care of your goldfish, you've purchase a book on proper goldfish care. We'll call it *The Goldfish Bible: Everything That Has Ever Been Learned about Goldfish for Their Proper Care, Happiness, and Longevity*. We'll be puzzled as to why this book never made any bestseller lists. At any rate, it tells you all about life in the fish-bowl.

As one deeply concerned with the health and well-being of your goldfish, you carefully read this book and follow all of its suggestions and instructions. Mr. Sloopy becomes a robust goldfish who swims giddily in circles and seems to possess telepathic powers. You tell your friends about your pet for hours at a time. They say they're quite happy for you even though they suddenly seem to have to be somewhere else, other than where you are.

One day, someone mentions a book filled with questions about life by some guy named Tim Pauls. You frown as you search your memory and then set them straight—you say, "I have to tell you that Tim Pauls doesn't exist, because there's no mention of him in *The Goldfish Bible*."

It's sad, but true—I'm not in there. But does that mean I don't exist? No! There's a reason I'm not in the book: I'm not in the fishbowl. That book is only about life in the bowl, and I'm outside of it. But I'm very much alive and well, thank you.

Now, picture the universe as the fishbowl and scientific knowledge as *The Goldfish Bible*. Science can tell us all sorts of incredible discoveries about this creation, about the heavens and the earth. But with one exception (see question 31), science can't tell you anything about God. Why? Because God is bigger than the fishbowl! He's the creator of the universe, not part of the creation. Since God is not a created being, He's not subject to the laws of science.

Many people believe that science and Scripture contradict each other. They do not! They are two different sources revealing different truths—Scripture primarily teaches us about God, while science teaches about His creation. It would be foolish to say, "Since the Bible doesn't speak of space travel, it's therefore impossible." The Bible doesn't say it's impossible; it simply doesn't talk about it. Likewise, it is just as foolish to say, "Since science can't prove

23

God, God doesn't exist." Remember, remember, remember: if science can't prove something, it means that—scientifically—it's neither true nor false. From science, we know that man can travel into space. From the Bible, we know that God exists.

God in the Fishbowl

Here's the part that confuses people—many people think and act as if, since God is the creator and not a created being, then the two remain separate. God remains way up in heaven where Scripture applies, while we remain in creation where science applies.

Not so! Even though God is greater than the universe—even though the Creator is beyond science, He still works within creation. It's not that He stays in heaven far, far away and has nothing to do with your life. He comes into the fishbowl. He works through His creation—and through science!—to care for all of your physical needs. He became flesh and died on the cross to save you from your sin. He comes to you, personally, in His Word and Holy Baptism and Holy Communion to give you the forgiveness He's won. This is where people get confused, because they don't expect God to be nearby; but the Lord remains "a very present help in trouble" (Psalm 46:1). This means that, sometimes in this world that normally runs by the laws of science, miracles happen. They happen because the Lord is here.

common sense

Here's the major limitation of common sense — it's a part of you, and you're sinful. This means that your common sense isn't completely trustworthy. It means that sometimes the wrong choice seems more sensible than the right one. It means that sometimes you'll make what's obviously the right decision, and then kick yourself later on because it was obviously the wrong decision. Common sense involves patiently studying options before making a decision. Above all, you must always make sure that your common sense does not contradict Scripture; if it does, you're the one who's wrong.

conscience

The same limitation is true for your conscience — since it also is part of you, therefore it is also sinful. Your conscience is designed to bother you when you do the wrong thing, but it's all too easy to dull your conscience by repeating a sin until it no longer bothers you. Like common sense, you must make sure your conscience follows Scripture. When it doesn't, it's time to repent.

The Queen of the Sciences

I think we've said enough to introduce our four witnesses of Scripture, science, common sense, and

25

conscience, except for one last thing: while all four are gifts of God to reveal truth to us, Scripture is a higher authority and source of truth than the rest. This makes sense: Scripture reveals God, the giver of science, common sense and conscience. The Creator is greater than the creation; therefore, the Bible—which reveals the truth about Him—is greater than the other witnesses which tell about what He has made.

That's why, back in history a ways, theology was known as the "Queen of the Sciences." To properly understand the universe, you first had to know about God. This remains true today. Be prepared, though, because many will scoff at the thought today and accuse you of trying to impose your Christianity on science. Those who don't believe in God often believe that science has disproved Him, even though it hasn't.

Anyway, enough with the introduction about the witnesses, here are some questions that often get asked about them.

26

1. How do i know that the Bible is true? **27**

You know the Bible is true because it says so, consider these Bible passages:

> All Scripture is breathed out by
> God and profitable for teaching,
> for reproof, for correction, and for
> training in righteousness.
> **(2 Timothy 3:16)**

> For no prophecy was ever produced
> by the will of man, but men spoke
> from God as they were carried along
> by the Holy Spirit. **(2 Peter 1:21)**

Time and time again, the Lord declares the Scriptures are His inspired Word.

2. That's not really proof. People say things that aren't true all the time.

That's not really a question either, but you're absolutely right. From day one, you're trained to demand proof and look for evidence—you want to have outside sources to support what people say. Part of this is because you've been trained to think scientifically, but there's another important reason—people lie a lot. Imagine this scene in a courtroom with an accused murderer on the witness stand:

> **Prosecutor:** We found you standing next to the body with the smoking gun in your hand and bloodstains on your clothes. Did you kill him?
>
> **Accused:** No.
>
> **Prosecutor:** Oh, okay, my mistake! Can I give you a ride home?

People lie a lot. That's one of the reasons we want witnesses to back up what they say. That's why, when you get around to buying a used car, you take it to a mechanic even if the salesman swears it's in good shape. That's why, when you apply for a job, the employer asks for references to tell about you—you haven't earned his trust yet. That's why, way back in the Old Testament, God required two or three witnesses before someone could be condemned, just in case one witness was lying (Deuteronomy 17:6).

However, when it comes to the Bible, keep these things in mind:

28

✱ God doesn't lie. His Word is always true, without error. Whatever He says is trustworthy. Therefore, He's the only One who doesn't need other witnesses to verify what He says.

✱ When you demand proof that the Bible is God's Word, you're trying to put the Bible into the science fishbowl. We already discussed why you can't do that.

✱ We can only believe God's Word through the power of God's Spirit. Without the Spirit the Word seems foolish (1 Corinthians 2:14).

✱ Just because there are no witnesses doesn't mean that someone isn't telling the truth. My name is my name, even if I'm in a room full of strangers who don't know who I am. Therefore, the fact that the Bible vouches for itself (the technical term for impressing your pastor is that the Bible is "self-authenticating") doesn't mean that it's lying. It simply means that science can't prove everything it says to be true—or false. The Bible is God's Word, it proclaims God's Word and will, which are above and beyond science. Although written down by men, it is authored by God (2 Timothy 3:16; 2 Peter 1:21)—so proving the authorship is something that science can't do.

29

3. So what should a scientist say about supernatural things?

An honest scientist will say, "If we can't prove something, then we can't confirm it or deny it." For example, some people will say that God doesn't exist because science can't prove that He does. However, science can't prove that He doesn't, either. True science therefore must admit that God might exist.

I get a kick out of our society. On the one hand, society wants to claim that God doesn't exist because science says so. On the other, society watches a lot of television about the paranormal and supernatural, because people are fascinated with the unexplainable. Have you noticed that we didn't list popular opinion or fads as witnesses?

It's worth repeating that science is a tool for examining the natural world—also known as creation, because God created things to run according to scientific laws. However, since God is the creator, not part of creation, then He's above and beyond science.

4. So if i can't prove that the Bible is God's Word, how do i know it's true?

You know this by faith. You believe it to be true because God says so. Consider Hebrews 11:1, "Now faith is the assurance of things hoped for, the conviction of things not seen," and 2 Corinthians 5:7, "for we walk by faith, not by sight." By definition, matters of faith can't be proven by science; if they could, they wouldn't be matters of faith! But this doesn't mean that they are untrue; it just means that they lie outside the realm of science.

So it is with the Bible: what it proclaims lies outside what is scientifically provable, but it's still true. So Jesus says to you, "Blessed are those who have not seen and yet have believed" (John 20:29).

5. Should we say that science deals with the "real world," but Scripture doesn't?

No. If Scripture doesn't deal with the real world, then it's just a fantasy story like *The Lord of the Rings*. Both Scripture and science deal with the real world, but each has a different purpose and focus. Science is God's gift for understanding how the natural world works in order to benefit our physical lives. But science has a limit—it can only study things that can be observed, tested, and repeated. The Bible declares God's interaction in this world for our eternal salvation; and since God is above and beyond science, the Bible won't fit into it.

Let's be clear: science is not an enemy of faith. We'll be using both Scripture and science to answer questions in this book. But it's very dangerous to make science the master over Scripture.

31

6. Are science and the Bible at cross-purposes with each other?

No, but they do have different purposes. The purpose of science is to learn about the creation around us. The purpose of the Bible is to teach us about Jesus. What St. John writes about his Gospel is true for all of Scripture: "But these are written so that you may believe that Jesus is the Christ, the Son of God, and that by believing you may have life in His name" (John 20:31).

If we respect that, science and Scripture can get along just fine. I don't use a whisk to mow my lawn, and I don't use a lawnmower to make scrambled eggs—each tool has its purpose. If I try to mow with a whisk, I'm going to conclude that it's good for nothing—but that's my fault, because I'm using it for the wrong purpose. Likewise, if I try to use science to explain God, it's not going to work very well. If I try to use the Bible to explain nuclear physics, I'm going to conclude that the Bible isn't helpful. That's not the fault of the Bible: it's my fault for using it for the wrong purpose.

7. Can you give some examples of making science the master over the Bible?

Yes, and this is important because you'll find people doing this all the time—and you'll especially find professors doing this in a lot of college classrooms. It's sometimes called rationalism, higher criticism, or historical criticism.

In general, the argument goes like this: whatever science can't verify in the Bible isn't true. Take, for example, this description of our Lord,

> "Jesus is the Son of God who became man and was born of the Virgin Mary. He taught people, performed all sorts of miracles and wonders, and died on the cross for the sins of the world. Three days later, He rose from the dead, ascended into heaven and will return to judge the living and the dead."

A historical critic will look at that summary, get out his marking pen, and cross out everything that science can't verify. When he's done, the summary looks like this:

> "Jesus was a man who lived, taught, and died."

See what this does? If you get rid of all the miraculous stuff, Jesus was just another guy. Shoot, I'm alive, I teach, and I'm going to die if the Lord doesn't return first. If that's all Jesus did, there's no hope.

Before we go further, look at that argument again—because it's not scientific! It doesn't follow the scientific method. Those who make the argument weren't there to observe Jesus. They can't test their hypothesis on Him because He's ascended into heav-

33

en, and they certainly can't repeat the test! Therefore, they can't prove that He didn't perform miracles.

By the way, people who buy into this preach some of the worst sermons. Imagine a pastor who doesn't believe in miracles, but he has to preach on Christmas, and his text is Luke 2:7: "And she gave birth to her firstborn son and wrapped Him in swaddling cloths and laid Him in a manger, because there was no place for them in the inn." Since this pastor doesn't believe that anything miraculous happened here, he's going to preach some lame sermon on proper care of newborn children, the art of swaddling, manger construction, or how hotels should always have rooms available if pregnant women drop by. Since none of this is particularly life-changing stuff, people stop coming to hear him preach. At this point, rather than repent, that pastor blames the Bible for being irrelevant, when he's the one who's gutted the message.

8. What does it mean when someone says that the Bible "contains" the Word of God?

Be really wary of that phrase. When somebody says that the Bible "contains" the Word of God, they usually mean that it also contains content that isn't the Word of God. Therefore, the Bible includes a mixture of God's Word and man's ideas, and it's up to you and me to figure out which is which. This allows people to keep the parts they like—which they decide is

God's Word, and get rid of the parts they don't like so much. This dangerous philosophy seeks to rob the Bible of authority. For instance, some scholars today claim that some of what St. Paul wrote was inspired by God; but when he condemns sexual immorality, it was just his personal opinion. Therefore, they claim, homosexuality and fornication are just fine with God. They will be terribly surprised on that scientifically unverifiable, yet very true day called the Final Judgment.

By the way, it's common to present this idea as "advanced theology." In other words, a professor who does this will tell you that he's there to give you a better understanding of the Bible by taking you past your "Sunday School" knowledge. "In Sunday School, it was okay to believe in miracles because you were just a kid. Now that you're older, it's time to get rid of believing in supernatural wonders; just like you grew up and stopped believing in Santa Claus, it's time to stop believing in Jesus as the Son of God." In other words it's time to stop believing in right and wrong. It's time to give up hoping for everlasting life. That's not growing up. It's abandoning the faith and inviting death!

Don't let someone bully you out of the faith by accusing you of being immature for trusting the Lord. Jesus has no problem with childlike faith: in fact, He praises it:

> Jesus declared, "I thank You, Father,
> Lord of heaven and earth, that You
> have hidden these things from the
> wise and understanding and revealed
> them to little children."
> **(Matthew 11:25)**

35

Whoever humbles himself like this child is the greatest in the kingdom of heaven. **(Matthew 18:4)**

9. Are there other ways the Bible comes under attack?

Sure. The devil uses all sorts of tricks used to convince you that the Bible isn't the Word of God. For instance, I remember someone telling me that the Israelites never worshiped a golden calf (like those found in Exodus 32:4 or 2 Kings 10:29) because archaeologists never found one. This is called an "argument of silence," which is bad logic—would you say, since you've never seen me, I don't exist? At any rate, guess what somebody dug up in the Middle East a few years back? Yup! A golden calf!

As another example, some argue that Genesis 1 and 2 were written by two different authors (not Moses, as the Bible says) because God is called by a different name in each; and no one would call God two different names, would he?

Let's think this through: if I call my wife "pumpkin" one day and "my little tulip bulb" the next, does that mean that I have two wives? Not at all! I just have one—one very patient wife who's wondering why I'd call her a type of squash.

Again, such an argument is very unscientific, because those making the argument weren't there to observe so they're only guessing. There are a ton of arguments like this out there; we simply don't have time in a book this size to cover them. However, you can use common sense to debunk a lot of them.

10. There's a lot at stake here, isn't there?

Absolutely! If you say that Scripture must agree with science to be true, you make science to be the master of Scripture. Then you lose salvation. You create a version of God that only acts in ways that we can measure and understand, rather than the Lord who, in His infinite wisdom, goes to the cross to save us from sin. You create a god smaller than your imagination. This is to create God in our image.

If the Bible remains the Word of God and His revelation of salvation, then you are blessed to have both the knowledge that God reveals in this world through science and the knowledge that He reveals in Scripture about His Son.

11. is this stuff popular?

Frankly, it's seen its day and it's on its way out— at least for now. However, it tends to thrive in university classrooms. If you're reading this, there's a good chance that college is in your near future. That's why I brought it up.

37

12. What is postmodernism?

Postmodernism is sort of the anti-science. It is an idea that teaches there is no such thing as absolute truth, and that it's up to you to determine what is true for you. Proof doesn't matter. Postmodernism would say, for instance, that if you believe premarital sex is okay, then it is; if you believe it's wrong, then it is. A few postmodernists might argue that 2+2=5 as long as you believe it.

Talk about dangerous! Many approach the Bible today with the idea that there's no such thing as truth, so it's up to you to decide what the Bible says. If you think a passage is true, then it's true. If you think it's false, then it's false. Do you see what this does? It puts you above God! It says that you'll decide when His Word is true and when it isn't. Your sinful nature loves this idea.

There's a great line in the movie *The Hitchhiker's Guide to the Galaxy* by Slartibartfast, who sums up postmodernism with one sentence: "I'd rather be happy than right." His next sentence says a lot, too. It's something like, "But I'm not happy, either, and that's where it all falls apart."

This is why postmodernism is already on its way out, too. As much as people like deciding what's true (a big part of being your own god), there are just too many things that are absolutely true, no matter what they believe. The biggest one is death; no matter how much people deny—they still die. Common sense is enough to refute postmodern thought.

13. is there more than one way to interpret the Bible?

Obviously, people have come up with all sorts of methods of interpreting the Bible. These different methods produce vastly different results. For instance, someone says, "I believe that God is only kind and never punishing. Therefore, I'm going to ignore any passage that describes Him as angry, and only use passages that make Him sound loving." So they read through the Bible, and guess what? He comes up with "proof" that God is only loving—not because the Bible says so—but because he said the Bible would say so before he started reading it!

Or, let's say that someone says, "Whenever I get to a part I don't understand, I'll guess what it means and trust that God made me guess right." This individual is going to come up with some pretty strange results, because he's relying on his imagination, not the Lord, to fill in the blanks.

When you read the Bible, beware of your preconceived notions, because you will try to use them to get the Bible to agree with you.

14. So is there a right way to interpret the Bible?

Yes! Allow me to illustrate. Let's say you hear me preach a sermon, and some of it is really clear. You don't need clarification on that part, because you know what I said. But there are a couple of things I

39

say that you find confusing. Who's the best person to ask? You could ask the guy next to you, but first you'd have to wake him up, and he might not know what I meant, either. No, the best thing to do is to ask me what I meant; then I can explain what wasn't clear before—that makes sense, too. But let's say that, after I explain it, it still doesn't click. At that point, you might be able to make an educated guess, but you still won't know for sure.

Now, apply this to interpreting the Bible.

> ✱ Where we clearly understand the Bible, we're going to speak with certainty. This makes sense.

> ✱ Where we don't clearly understand a passage in the Bible, we're going to look around for help in the Bible. This makes sense, too: if you don't understand what the Lord says, who should you ask? Him! So we look for answers where He speaks to us—in His Word.

> ✱ If we do all the investigating we can and still don't clearly understand the passage, we're going to admit it and say, "We don't know." We can make an educated guess, but we're not going to say, "This is most certainly true." We're not going to say, "You must believe what we're not sure of." Our dinky minds aren't going to understand everything about God.

15. is the Bible ever unclear?

No, and that's where the analogy I just used breaks down. (With analogies, sooner or later, they teach the wrong thing if you keep pushing and trying to find more comparisons than were intended.) In using the illustration of one of my sermons to God's Word, there's a really important distinction—if you don't understand something in my sermon, it is very possible that I have been unclear. If we don't understand something in God's Word, it is not that God has failed to be clear, but that our finite, sin-confused minds can't comprehend it. There's a good reason that St. Paul writes, "Oh, the depth of the riches and wisdom and knowledge of God! How unsearchable are His judgments and how inscrutable His ways!" (Romans 11:33)

41

16. Does that even need to be said?

It does, because some have made this argument: "God wouldn't put anything in the Bible that we couldn't understand; therefore, we should be able to understand everything in it." To this, we apply our witnesses.

First, the Word of God: where in Scripture does it promise that we'll be able to understand everything in the Bible? It doesn't. It does warn, however, that knowledge puffs up (1 Corinthians 8:1) and that we should guard against pride.

Second, common sense: If God is infinitely wise,

and our minds are finite and clouded with sin to one degree or another, can we expect to understand everything God says in His Word? Hardly!

And so Deuteronomy 29:29 seals the deal:

> The secret things belong to the Lord our God, but the things that are revealed belong to us and to our children forever, that we may do all the words of this law.

17. Do Christians really follow every law in the Bible? i mean, when was the last time you sacrificed an animal at church?

No, we don't sacrifice animals at church, even though I'm sorely tempted when it comes to the woodpecker that interrupts many worship services here. This is a very important point: there are all sorts of laws in the Old Testament that Christians don't follow anymore. We don't sacrifice animals, throw lepers out of town, or conduct certain mildew tests. So how come we keep some laws, ignore others, yet claim that we follow the Bible? And how come we keep the laws that we do?

Here's your answer: "For when there is a change in the priesthood, there is necessarily a change in the law as well" (Hebrews 7:12).

Just in case that didn't send shivers up your spine, let's unpack it. Back in the Old Testament, while the people of God were still waiting for the Savior to be born, they had a central place of worship—first the tabernacle, then the temple in Jerusalem. The rituals of the temple were conducted by the priests, and the priests had to be men who were members of the tribe of Levi. Therefore, it was called the levitical priesthood. The priests would offer the sacrifices, and the high priest would enter the Holy of Holies—into the presence of God—once a year.

Along with the temple and the priests, God gave a bunch of laws about worship and everyday life. You can find the majority of these in the book of Leviticus—here's the kicker—the levitical priests were in charge of the levitical law that you find in Leviticus. See the theme? The laws and the priests went together.

43

One of the big points of the book of Hebrews is this—Jesus is our High Priest. He offered the sacrifice for our sin even as He was the sacrifice for our sin. He entered into His Father's presence to intercede for us. Jesus isn't a levitical priest. As God, He's the Son of God. As man, He was born to Mary, who was of the tribe of Judah—not Levi. Since we have Jesus as our High Priest, we don't need levitical priests anymore.

Now here's the last piece of the puzzle—levitical law went with levitical priests. If we're no longer under levitical priests, then we're no longer under the law that went with them. That's why we don't sacrifice animals anymore. Not to mention the fact that, since Jesus shed His blood on the cross for us, there aren't any sacrifices left to be made!

So which laws do we keep? The laws of our new High Priest. We keep the laws that Jesus renews in the New Testament—either by His own teaching in the Gospels or by His chosen New Testament writers in their epistles. He repeats that murder is wrong (Matthew 5:20–21), so we still declare "Thou shalt not kill." He doesn't repeat the command not to shave the sides of your head (Leviticus 19:27), so you don't have to grow your hair long.

That's how we determine which laws still apply and which ones don't. We listen to our Savior in the New Testament.

We are moved to keep these laws as a joyful response to the gift of God's grace and forgiveness.

18. Are the Ten Commandments still in effect? And can i work on Sundays?

The Ten Commandments are still in effect to the extent that Jesus says they are. Here's an example.

When the Lord originally commanded, "Remember the Sabbath day, to keep it holy" (Exodus 20:8), He added that no one should do any work on that day. In Old Testament Israel, virtually all labor ceased on the seventh day. (Ironically, the priests were the ones who worked on the Sabbath!) This day of rest was to remind the people God created the world in six days and rested on the seventh (Exodus 20:9–11). It was also intended to point toward Jesus, who brings rest and peace between God and man (Hebrews 4:4–16).

During His public ministry, Jesus set this aside, declaring "The Sabbath was made for man, not man for the Sabbath. So the Son of Man is lord even of the Sabbath" (Mark 2:27–28; see also Colossians 2:16–17). In Jesus' time, the Pharisees believed that salvation came through good works, that they impressed God by not working on the Sabbath. Jesus set aside this part of the commandment, telling them to look to the Son of Man for salvation. Some today still insist that it is sinful for a Christian to work on Sunday, be it mowing the lawn or flipping burgers for pay. This just isn't so—the point of the Third Commandment, as the Small Catechism declares, is that "We should fear and love God that we do not despise preaching and His Word, but hold it sacred and gladly hear and learn it" (SC p. 12). Clearly, the Lord still commands us to hear and obey His Word (John 14:23); and as we do so, remember from the Sabbath rest that it was the Lord who did all the work to save us from sin.

Other than this, the Lord renews the Ten Commandments. You are still forbidden to have other gods before Him (Matthew 4:10) and to take His name in vain (James 2:7). You are not to kill (Matthew 5:21–22), commit adultery (Matthew 5:27–28), steal (Romans 13:9), bear false witness (Matthew 5:33–37), or covet (Romans 7:7).

And, of course, don't forget: you're still supposed to honor your parents (Matthew 15:4).

19. Where do emotions fit in as a witness?

Popular opinion leads us to believe that it's a good thing to follow your feelings, to do something because "it just feels right." This isn't a good idea. Sometimes, the wrong thing feels right and the right thing feels wrong.

Don't get me wrong, emotions are a part of who we are, a part of who God created us to be. Like conscience and common sense, though, feelings are corrupted by sin and can lead you astray pretty badly.

There's a big way that emotions aren't like conscience and common sense. Conscience and common sense deal with objective truths. They both deal with what is true and false, right and wrong. Emotions aren't like that, they're subjective. They don't reflect right and wrong. Instead, they reflect how much you like something, whether it's right or wrong. Quick test—which thrills you more—watching your favorite television show or studying for the math exam? On the night before the test, which is the better thing to do?

Furthermore, emotions change depending on mood, energy, and circumstance. On my drive to the church each morning, there's one big, busy intersection with a stoplight, and the stoplight is often red for my side street when I get there. When it's red, it makes objective sense to stop. Look at what the witnesses say:

Scripture: you should obey the laws of the land, so stop.

Science: the laws of physics say that if you try to occupy the same space at the same time as that city bus that's roaring through, you're going to get hurt; so stop.

Common sense: along with the bus argument, it would be chaos if people ignored traffic signals, so stop.

Conscience: even if you don't get hurt running the red light, you're going to feel bad about doing it. Stop!

See! Every witness of right and wrong agrees, not one of them is going to change. However, my emotions about this particular stoplight will change. If I need to jot a quick note in my PDA, I might be thankful that the light is red to give me time. If I'm well-rested and not particularly stressed, the stoplight doesn't bother me. But if I'm short on sleep or worrying about something, I'm going to be impatient, even angry at a stoplight. Do you see? My emotions change, even though it's the same stoplight.

This is what emotions do, they change based upon a whole bunch of factors. They're not about right and wrong. That doesn't make them bad, it just means you can't say, "I know this is true and right because it feels right."

20. What about experience as a witness? Don't i learn from what i've experienced in life?

Yes—and no—it all depends. Here's what I mean.

Experience can be a great teacher, when our four witnesses are doing the teaching. Let's say you do something stupid . . . you back your parents' car into a post. Common sense tells you to watch your mirrors better, the science of economics tells you it's going to take a while to pay for the damage, and your conscience won't let you forget it for a while. In this case, you're learning objective stuff from experience, because the witnesses make use of it to teach you right and wrong.

However, without the witnesses, experience becomes a bad teacher. Why? Because people naturally believe that their experiences are universal and complete. Here's what I mean: I had a conversation with a guy who was checking out our congregation. He wasn't a Christian, but he knew he was missing something. In our conversation, he related how his first contact with Christianity had been a hospital chaplain who had spoken about "God's love" while playing secular oldies tunes on his guitar. The chaplain never mentioned Jesus or forgiveness, just how God loved everybody and let's all sing "You Are My Sunshine, My Only Sunshine." Based on that experience, for a long time, this guy decided that all Christian pastors were guitar-playing doofuses who really didn't have anything important to say.

I object to that generalization. I am not a guitar-playing doofus. I do not play the guitar.

This is called arguing from the particular to the general. Because one pastor was off-track, all pastors are off-track. Because one Yankees fan was obnoxious, all Yankees fans are obnoxious. Because one guy with an accent wouldn't talk to me, all foreigners are sinister and up to no good. This is a bad way to operate—it goes against common sense and puts your personal perceptions and emotions above the witnesses.

The other thing about experience is that it comes from interacting with other people. Other sinful people. This means that what they do is not necessarily in keeping with God's Word. Here's a standard exchange between a parent and child that you hear all the time (well, at least in my experience):

> **CHILD:** Aw, mom, why can't I go to the party? It's just a few friends drinking alcohol and running across the launch pad just before the shuttle blasts off. Everybody else is going.

> **MOM:** If everybody else jumped off a cliff, would you do that, too?

Now, you and I know that everybody else isn't going. Even if they were, it doesn't make it right. But experience is used like that to justify all sorts of stuff. Just look at how the news treats some sins: Lots of people smoke marijuana, so it must be okay. Lots of teens are having sex; therefore, it must be fine.

49

As a pastor, my favorite one is this: "Pastor, we should do this because the church down the street is doing it." If the church down the street jumped off a cliff . . . well, you know. Whether it's illicit drugs or changing worship, the deciding factor isn't what other people do. The deciding factor isn't what we've enjoyed in our experience. The deciding factor is what we learn from our four witnesses, and God has the final say in His Word.

Sometimes, people believe in absolute truth. You don't run across many who say, "As long as I believe the tank is full, my car won't run out of gas." You don't run across them because they're stranded alongside the roadway somewhere, wondering why their faith let them down.

Sometimes, people like certain guarantees. They don't like to be unsure. It's a lot more comfortable to be certain you've got a date, you're accepted into college or that you've got the job. When it comes to things that matter, people want to be sure.

And when it comes to scientific things, people seem pretty happy when science gives definitive, certain answers.

But when it comes to God, our old sinful nature kicks in. People don't want to be so sure anymore. "Can we really be sure that immorality is still sinful?" "Can we really be sure that Jesus is the only way to heaven?" "Can we really be certain that God created the heavens and the earth in six, 24-hour days?" Such questions go back a long way: how did the devil begin tempting Adam and Eve? He said, "Did God actually say . . . ?" (Genesis 3:1).

Because of sin, people—you and me included—always want to question God's Word. We take issue with what He has to say. The devil delights in this, because such doubt makes it easier for him to lead you back into sin and death. Don't be fooled into believing that God's Word isn't absolute truth, that you can make it say whatever you want.

In fact, rejoice that God's Word is absolute truth and doesn't change. That means it is always true that the Lord has redeemed you by His death on the cross. It means that it is always true that He works all things for your good (Romans 8:28). It means that it is always true that, in Christ, heaven is yours. Your health and happiness and financial situation will come and go, rise and fall. Little in this life is certain. But as you ponder the questions in the rest of this book, and as you wrestle with other issues where the answer isn't always clear, thank God that you can be sure of His unfailing love for you. He's bought you with the price of His Son's blood, and He will never abandon you. This is most certainly true.

52 Section Two: Creator & Creation

Every section of this book starts out with some notes before the questions, information that applies in general to all the questions that follow. This is the shortest section of notes, though, because I've given you most of what you need in Section 1.

However, many of the following questions have to

do with creation and evolution. There are lots of books about evolution, both for and against it, in bookstores today. They often are many pages long and not particularly thrilling. Maybe it's just me, but I really don't want to read several pages on how the chromosomes of a fruit fly prove that we all came from soup, then spend the rest of my life learning about genetics so I can prove the chapter wrong. This is one of the reasons why evolution can be difficult, and annoying, to refute. If you're going to debate all the details, then you have to be an expert in astronomy, chemistry, geology, biology, microbiology, and more. This is why evolutionists seem to have the upper hand. Like the historical critics we talked about in the section on witnesses, they can drown you with technical stuff few people understand enough to argue against.

So let's not worry about the technical details. For our purposes here, all you need to know are the following four truths that apply to everything in the scientific world. If evolution doesn't agree with these, then all the little details don't matter. This would be like worrying about floor mats when your car doesn't have an engine.

the four truths

1. To prove something scientifically, you have to use the scientific method. Review Section 1 if you want more information, but remember: in the world of science, you have to observe something,

53

test your guess about it, and repeat the test. If you can't do these things, you can't arrive at a scientific theory.

2. If you can't prove something scientifically, it doesn't mean it's false. It doesn't mean it's true. It means that, in terms of science, it remains an unknown.

3. According to the First Law of Thermodynamics, nothing comes from nothing. Things don't spontaneously appear in science—they always have an origin.

4. According to the Second Law of Thermodynamics, things fall apart. They go from order to disorder. This is called entropy. If you drop a coffee cup, it shatters. If you pick up the pieces and drop them again, they do not turn back into a coffee cup. If you want a more scientific example, scientists tell us that, eventually, the sun is going to burn out. It's not going to get brighter and stronger. Why? Technically, because things go from order to disorder. Because things always fall apart. They die. That's entropy, and it's the law.

That's what you need to know, so let's talk about the world. We've got to start answering questions about life somewhere, so the beginning seems like a good spot.

21. How do we know that God exists?

I suppose I could just say, "Because the Bible says so," and quote something like Genesis 1:1, "In the beginning, God created the heavens and the earth." Honestly, that's good enough for me; however, there's a good chance you're asking that question because you're wondering if we have any evidence besides the Bible. It's not that the Bible isn't good enough; rather, you want some ammunition for those who aren't going to listen to Scripture.

Actually, Genesis 1:1 points us in the right direction, because it tells us that the heavens and the earth were made by God. You see, it's a law of science that everything has to come from something in the natural world. In other words, carrots don't just "poof" into being, but grow from seeds. Cars don't suddenly appear; they're made in factories. According to the laws of physics (like the First Law of Thermodynamics), nothing comes from nothing, and everything comes from something. Trees come from seeds that come from trees. The chicken came from an egg that came from a chicken. My seventh grade science teacher was beamed down from the mother ship. Well, that was the rumor, anyway.

So, where did the heavens and the earth come from? Everything in science says they had to come from something . . . or Someone. Scientifically, creation has to have a source—according to science, it can't be any other way. Psalm 14:1 kicks in and says, "The fool says in his heart, 'There is no God.'" It's illogical to think otherwise.

22. So is evolution a scientific fact?

It's not even close. Remember the method used for science: you observe something, form a hypothesis, test your guess, and repeat the test. According to evolutionists, no one was around to observe the initial eons of evolution. (In fact, a lot more people witnessed the resurrected Jesus! See 1 Corinthians 15:5–8. How come evolutionists aren't lining up to insist that it's true?) Since changes happen extremely gradually over gigantic amounts of time, there is no way to test evolution and no way to repeat the test. Evolution isn't fact. It doesn't even deserve to be called a theory, because it hasn't been proven.

By the way, we're talking about macro-evolution here. Micro-evolution, that concept that species can change and adapt over time, is a whole different discussion.

23. What is theistic evolution?

Theistic evolution is the idea that God created everything, but used evolution to do it. Therefore, as the argument goes, the "days" of creation in Genesis 1 don't refer to literal, 24-hour days, but to different spans of time lasting millions of years each. This is an attempt to make the Bible agree with the so-called "theory" of evolution. This is an attempt to make science king over Scripture, but still let the Bible have a place. In other words, a theistic evolutionist says, "I believe science is true for sure, so we have to edit the Bible to make it agree."

In the ground rules earlier in this book, we said we weren't going to operate that way.

The Bible simply doesn't permit theistic evolution. I don't want to bore you with the arguments, but the text of Genesis 1 makes clear that the heavens and earth were created in six, literal, 24-hour days; and nowhere does God's Word suggest otherwise.

24. So what? Why does it matter how God created the heavens and the earth?

It matters because salvation is at stake. You see, if you let some bad science persuade you that the Bible is wrong in Genesis 1, you've opened the door that the Bible could be wrong in all sorts of places. It could be wrong that Jesus is the Son of God, born of Mary. It could be wrong that He died for your sins and rose again. If Genesis 1 isn't true, how do you know for sure that the Gospels will be? To deny God's truth is a serious sin, because the Lord declares that those who do not hear and believe His Word are not of God (John 8:47).

25. But doesn't scientific evidence show that the earth is really, really old?

You can read a lot of books about different ways of measuring the age of the earth, like carbon-14 dating, and so forth. (I once tried to date Carbon 14, but she was seeing somebody else.) In the introduction to this book, I already said I'd answer these questions as a pastor, so let me ask you this: on the day they were created, how old were Adam and Eve? Were they newborn babies, little blobs that lay on the ground and waited to grow up? Of course not. They were full grown adults. God created them as mature adults. At the age of one day, they were all grown up. I've never heard any Christian say otherwise. (I do remember one guy arguing that, since God created us in His image, and we start out as a one-cell zygote, God must be a single-cell amoeba kind of thing out there. Sounds like a really bad Star Trek episode to me. I think the guy was a little bit off.)

So if God could create mature people, why couldn't He create a mature universe? Why couldn't He create heavens and earth that looked like they'd been around for a while?

Answer: He most certainly could have. Why would He? For our good. Here's just one example that comes to mind, and I'm freely admitting it's just speculation on my part. Scientists say that fossil fuels (oil, coal, natural gas) took millions of years to develop. Now, I'm quite happy to believe that the Lord created a mature earth with a lot of oil reserves in place, rather than making us wait a few more millennia before we can fill up the car.

Likewise, astronomers will argue that the universe is millions of years old because it would take that long for light from distant stars to reach the earth; since we can see the stars, they've been around for a while. However, why couldn't God create stars where their light already extended for millions of miles? He could. He did!

The Lord didn't make the heavens and the earth to be new; He created them to be a blessing to Adam and Eve. He created a mature creation for their good.

26. i heard someone say that the fact that animals have such similar DNA is proof of evolution, evidence that all animals came from an original, common organism.

Let's use common sense on this one. Isn't that similar DNA just as much a proof that all animals were created by the same God?

For instance, imagine that you're walking through an art museum, and an entire wall is covered with paintings. As you examine them, you note that each painting is different. However, each one has similar lighting, brush technique, and use of color. Many of them are variations on the same theme. What do you conclude? That the paintings all came from the same artist—not that they're an accident. Likewise, why wouldn't different animals, created by the same God, have similar DNA? (By the way, Ephesians 2:10 says, "we are His workmanship, created in Christ Jesus for good works, which God prepared beforehand, that we should walk in them." In Greek the word for "workmanship" is the word from which we get "poem." You are God's poem, His work of art.)

27. is there life on other planets?

The Bible doesn't say that there is, but the Bible doesn't say that there isn't. Science hasn't found any, either. From the sound of Genesis 1 and 2, my hunch is that there isn't life on other planets. I wouldn't completely rule out some sort of mold clinging to a rock somewhere; but I don't lie awake at night worried that interstellar goldfish are going to show up and vaporize the earth, either.

28. if some sort of organism were found on other planets, would it mean the Bible was wrong?

No, because the Bible doesn't say there isn't any life on other planets.

29. How do i deal with evolution in science class at school?

61

This is a pretty serious concern especially for a lot of Christian teens who attend public school. You don't want give the appearance you approve of evolution by remaining silent; yet on the other hand, your teacher may not be real keen on you bringing up God during science class.

Most science teachers tend to really, really like students who do more than spit out answers on a test. If you're being tested on principles of evolution, you could do more than answer the question—you could give some additional data to disprove the principles. For instance, imagine a test question says, "Explain the basics of the Big Bang Theory." Having studied diligently for hours the night before, you write about how "Edwin Hubble noted that the universe was expanding and thus proposed that, at one time, all matter had been in the same place before exploding outward, blah, blah, blah." After you finish this brilliant and articulate answer, you then add, "Of course, Mr. Hubble could not explain where all of that material came from in the first place, even though the laws of science would say it had to come from somewhere. This still remains a mystery to science today, one that the Big Bang Theory cannot explain." You've now answered the question and pointed out a big weakness in the theory, even though you've remained scientific the whole time. You might even get extra credit!

Beware of an unnecessary pitfall. I have come across students who felt it their duty to answer that same question by saying, "The Big Bang Theory is wrong, because God created the heavens and the earth." They fail the question—not because they've said something false, nor because they're being persecuted. They fail the question because they didn't answer it. If I were their teacher, I'd count it wrong too.

30. Should i really write "blah, blah, blah" on a science test?

No.

31. Does science teach us anything about God?

Yes it does. Science actually says that God, or at least a god, exists. The First Law of Thermodynamics says that nothing comes from nothing. Therefore, the universe had to come from something—or someone. Therefore, there's a god out there somewhere. It's scientifically impossible that there's always been a bunch of matter floating around that exploded into a universe. In other words, the fact there is a creation is evidence there is a creator.

Given this information, we can also deduce other things, like the Creator is powerful, immensely intelligent, and creative.

32. What is "intelligent design"?

63

"Intelligent design" is the idea—are you ready for this?—someone intelligent designed the universe. In a few places around the nation, people are proposing that, along with the "theory" of evolution, students also learn the theory this universe is the product of an intelligent being or beings. Even though God isn't specifically mentioned in the proposal of intelligent design, opponents claim this movement is simply an underhanded attempt by Christians to get religion and creation back into the classroom. Therefore, they oppose students learning there might be another opinion besides evolution.

Maybe I'm just one of those underhanded Christians, but shouldn't a true scientist allow other theories in? I mean, people could introduce the idea intelligent design, discuss it and then prove how it's wrong. Except it can't be proven wrong, and it's a lot more reasonable than evolution.

33. Didn't God have to come from somewhere?

According to science, God had to come from somewhere; but God isn't controlled by the laws of science! Ask an evolutionist what got evolution going, and they may well say the Big Bang did it. Okay, what caused the Big Bang to, uh, bang in such a big way? They can't answer because they don't know: the answer doesn't lie within science.

The Bible declares God is eternal (1 Timothy 1:17). He has always been and always will be. This doesn't fit in with science; however, use some common sense here. If everything comes from something, it only makes sense there is something eternal to get the ball rolling. It couldn't be any other way. Hebrews 11:3 says, "By faith we understand that the universe was created by the word of God, so that what is seen was not made out of things that are visible."

34. Okay, so we know that God exists. How do we know who God is?

That's what you can't learn from science. Common sense will tell you He's out there somewhere, and your conscience will tell you He's made some laws you've violated; because if He and His laws didn't exist, you wouldn't feel bad about breaking them. But as far as who God is, that's a question answered by the Bible alone, because that's where He reveals who He is. It's in Scripture you find His name, His identity, and His plan of salvation for you in Christ. There are some excellent books which summarize what the Bible says, not the least of which is *Luther's Small Catechism*; so rather than repeat what they already say, I'll direct you to them.

The big point I want to make here is this: you know who God is because He tells you who He is in His Word. You don't have to guess or speculate.

35. Does it really matter who God is? Can't we call God anything we want?

Before we pull out the big guns of Scripture on this one, let's use a little common sense. You have a name and an identity: you are who you are. So let's say some high school student named Noah Michaels introduces himself to me and says, "Hi, I'm Noah Michaels and I'm a high school student." I reply, "No, I believe you're actually Zooey the Squidboy from outer space." Who is right? Obviously, I'm not. I can call him Zooey the Squidboy all I want, but he's still Noah Michaels, high school student—even if he does have tentacles, and squirts radioactive ink when he gets mad—weird!

The point is, what I believe doesn't make something what it is. Noah doesn't become Zooey because I say so. Carrots don't become peas because I believe it. God doesn't change to fit my beliefs. Rather, He tells us who He is specifically and gives us faith to believe it.

One more illustration: let's say you and I are talking one day, and you mention a guy named Nathan Christopher. "Nathan Christopher?" I say. "I know Nathan Christopher, too. And if you ever need help in math, he's the guy to see." You remember this; and when you're having trouble with algebra, you give him a call. He meets with you and you spend a whole day studying math. The following day, you fail the test miserably. I mean, you really bomb. What happened? As it turns out, we were talking about two different guys named Nathan Christopher. The one I know is a math whiz; the one you know adds 2+2 and comes up with "blue" for his answer. The point of this is simple: a lot of people say they believe in Jesus, but they believe He's different than the Bible says. Somewhere along the way, they believe in a different Jesus entirely, one who can't save them. Where do they cross the line? I don't know for sure. God knows, but no one else can.

So, yes; it matters who God says He is. If you give Him a different name and believe He's different than He says He is, guess what? You've got a different god instead. No other god can save because no other god has gone to the cross and died to take away your sins.

36. What is universalism?

Universalism is the idea all religions lead to the

same place, everybody gets to heaven. God wears different masks and demands different things for different people, but the one true God is behind the scenes in any kind of faith people come up with. Therefore, apparently, an atheist is saved by denying God and the possibility of eternal life. This philosophy is very popular today for a couple of reasons. First, this way nobody has to be wrong. If the same God is at work in every religion, we can be happy for everybody and even mix up different religions into a spiritual casserole. (When different religions start mixing and worshiping together, it's called syncretism.) Second, whether or not people will admit it, this idea lets them be the god. They decide which religion is good for them. They decide which parts they have to obey. In other words, they get to tell their god what to do.

The one true God puts a stop to all of this with the First Commandment, "You shall have no other gods before Me" (Exodus 20:3). Literally, "before Me" means "before My face." "In My sight" would be a pretty close parallel. In Isaiah 42:8, God declares, "I am the Lord; that is My name; My glory I give to no other, nor My praise to carved idols."

Speaking of making sense, let's put some common sense to work here. Most religions have unique teachings which exclude others: for instance, if you believe you're saved because Jesus died on the cross to take away your sins (Christianity), then Islam must be wrong when it teaches you're saved by doing enough works and keeping enough rules. Both can't be true, right? Yet universalists and syncretists will argue that each religion should give up whatever teachings disagree with the rest in order to compromise. Therefore, in arguing all religions are good, they show they don't take any religion seriously! Again, this is attractive to sinners because it lets them determine what is true. Or, rather, what they think is true.

37. The Bible says that God is male. What about feminist theology, which says that God is at least partly female?

Feminist theology claims God is either both male and female or even strictly female. However, without bogging down on this point, feminist theologians also practice the following principles for building their beliefs:

> ✷ There is no such thing as special revelation. In other words, the Bible isn't the Word of God.

> ✷ Therefore, religion is built out of the experience of men and women, not God's Word. (We already warned about experience as a reliable witness in question 20.)

> ✷ Since God doesn't speak in His Word, people have the freedom to define reality, self and God. People get to decide who God is. Behind all the fancy arguments, feminists

declare God is female only because they want to believe it, not because it's true.

❋ According to feminism, the goal of Christianity is not to give out the forgiveness of sins, but to free women from oppression.

See any problems? No matter their intentions, feminist theologians want to turn Christianity into a religion that denies the Word, the identity of God and the forgiveness of sins! Where there is no forgiveness of sins, there is neither life, nor salvation.

38. is environmentalism good or bad?

The environmentalist movement is dedicated to preserving nature. Is it good or bad? It depends.

Here's the "good" side, "And God blessed [Adam and Eve]. And God said to them, 'Be fruitful and multiply and fill the earth and subdue it and have dominion over the fish of the sea and over the birds of the heavens and over every living thing that moves on the earth'" (Genesis 1:28). Right from the beginning, God entrusted Adam and Eve with the earth. It was given to them to take care of it and preserve it. Note that they were to "have dominion" over the earth. Adam and Eve weren't just another part of creation like gophers or coconut trees. They were created in the image of God—they were the crown jewel of creation. They were people with souls, valued by God more than all the rest. As descendants of Adam and

Eve, we still have the responsibility of taking care of this earth for as long as we can. It's going to end someday, but that's no excuse. My car is going to stop working someday, too, but I still change the oil. Part of our vocation, our calling, on earth is to take care of the earth as best we can. In fact, since the world is going to fall apart (see the Second Law of Thermodynamics), it makes sense that we do our best to be good stewards. In that sense, it's good for us to take care of the environment. I'm all for clean air, clean water, recycling, and other responsible measures.

39. When does environmentalism become a bad thing?

Consider this, "Claiming to be wise, they became fools, and exchanged the glory of the immortal God for images resembling mortal man and birds and animals and reptiles" (Romans 1:22–23). Because of the fall into sin, people have a tendency to worship created things. In fact, some people worship nature and the earth; sometimes called paganism or neo-paganism. Wicca (modern-day witchcraft) is a pretty close cousin.

Here's how it goes: people don't want to believe in God, so they deny He exists. On the other hand, they realize that they're pretty puny and can't keep themselves alive, so there must be something greater than them to rely on. Since they've already rejected the Creator, what's left for them to trust in? The creation! God the Father gets replaced by "Mother

Earth" or "Mother Nature." But the earth is not your mother. It did not give birth to you, and you do not owe it parental honor.

Here's where environmentalism gets scary. A lot of environmentalism is based upon the idea that God isn't there to take care of us, so this planet is all that we've got. Therefore, we must defend the planet at all costs from all threats. Environmentalism sees people both as the greatest threat to nature and the only hope to keep it going. The most obvious example of this is radical environmentalism, where someone chooses to live in a tree for months or years to prevent it from being cut down; or eco-terrorism, where terrorists destroy buildings and equipment in order to prevent human activity in wilderness areas.

So there's what makes environmentalism good or bad—when people take care of the creation as part of their service to God who entrusted it to them, it's a good thing. When people take care of the creation because they believe there's no creator and it's up to them to keep the world going, it denies God and becomes a bad thing.

71

40. Why are there so many arguments about the environment?

Dealing with the environment isn't an easy thing, because you've got to balance a bunch of different needs. Here in the west, we have hydroelectric dams that generate a lot of electricity for a bunch of states. However, these dams hinder the salmon from migrating upstream and reproducing. You make the call: should we risk killing off all the salmon and keep powering the west coast; or should we destroy the dams, save the fish and live by candlelight? For another example, if everyone stopped driving cars, the air would be cleaner; but I think motorized transportation is worth it, don't you?

Here's the challenge—you and I need to do our best to use our resources in ways that best serve those alive today and those who are yet to be born. This won't be an easy thing, because this world is wearing out. Thanks to sin, it's not going to last forever. (The Second Law of Thermodynamics strikes again!)

41. is Gaia theory related to this?

You might come across Gaia theory in college. It has a lot of different variations. At the tame end, it's essentially the idea that all living parts of nature affect each other as they operate in order to keep life going. At the other end, it gets strange and religious. First, think about your body, which we'll call "Planet You." You've got a bunch of systems all working together to keep you going. Your stomach is digesting and your kidneys are cleansing. Your nervous system is sensing and your liver is filtering. Add all of these parts together, and they equal "Planet You." In addition to all of that, there are also those tiny mites, bacteria, and parasites that scientists like to magnify in textbooks to creep you out. Like it or not, they're on "Planet You," too.

Gaia theory doesn't say that your body is a planet. Instead, it says that the earth is an organism, a living body. All the different plants and animals, along with tides and storms and volcanoes, are different parts and processes that keep the "body" going. This is where Gaia theory is a good friend of environmentalism: it's important to keep every kind of plant and animal alive because they all support and serve the larger body—earth.

In Gaia theory, you're not much. You and I are simply small organisms that live in the body and contribute to it as we can. Eventually we die, serving the body as fertilizer, and that's the end of us. I'm sure you see the problem with this theory. Instead of being created in God's image and redeemed by Christ, you're kind of a parasite on the way to the compost heap and nothing more.

Is Gaia theory far out? It's pretty strange, but it's worth talking about now because it's another teaching that tends to thrive better on college campuses than elsewhere in the world. You'll come across it sooner or later.

Ideas like Gaia theory and evolution are depressing to me, because they both show how far people will go to deny the existence of God—and how sin tricks them into running away from hope. The cure for my sadness, however, is a Bible verse we say just about every Sunday at church as part of the liturgy, "Our help is in the name of the Lord, Who made heaven and earth" (Psalm 124:8). The same Lord who created the universe also sent His Son to redeem you and me from sin, by His death on the cross. You're not

73

an accidental development, just one result of a mind-less explosion billions of years ago. You're not a germ on the host planet who serves by fertilizing after you die.

You're the careful creation of an intelligent, all-knowing God. You're fearfully and wonderfully made (Psalm 139:14), not a random accident. More than that, He so loves and values you that He's redeemed you at the cost His Son's own blood. Because He lives, you will live also forever. Now, that's hope. And because it's God's promise, it's a certain hope.

74

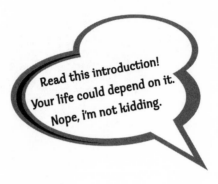

Read this introduction! Your life could depend on it. Nope, i'm not kidding.

Section Three: Matters of Life and Death

Anytime people reject God, they start treating life as something really cheap and disposable. This is already a big problem—it's not going to get any better soon.

If you're a teenager, then you should know that everybody wants to be like you. This may come as a surprise. For a couple years in junior high, I didn't even want to be like me. But it's true. Look at the commercials on television, and you'll see a common theme emerge from a bunch of them. This product gets rid of fine lines and wrinkles, while that one keeps hair from looking gray. This one firms skin, that one helps hair look thicker, more youthful. Then, of course, there are the hideous, "subtle" commercials for Viagra and Levitra (wink-wink, nudge-nudge), not to mention the vitamin commercials that show senior citizens on long-range bike trips or lifting buses over their heads. Do you notice a theme yet? When was the last time you saw a commercial where the model boasted, "When I use this cream, I look ten years older!"?

We might as well mention that plastic surgery, microderm abrasion, and Botox® injections are a huge industry, and that fitness products are selling fast, too.

There's one more immensely disturbing trend. Middle-aged adults trying to dress like teenagers. While wearing a crop-top is normally immodest; for some who aren't so youthful, it really ought to be a crime.

You've probably figured it out by now—everyone wants to be like you—they want to be young. They want to stay young. Americans are repulsed by the prospect of growing old, which is quite unfortunate because it's rather unavoidable. It's like running on a treadmill that never stops going the other way.

Why are so many people obsessed with staying young? In my opinion, it comes down to one word:

entropy. The good old Second Law of Thermo-dynamics works on the human body, too. The older we get, the more things don't work so well. This also means that the older we get, the closer we are to death.

That, in my opinion, is why America is obsessed with youth—because of the fear of death.

Now, I'm a Christian with the certain hope of eter-nal life, because Jesus has redeemed me at the cross and made me His own in Holy Baptism. Even though heaven is mine, I'll be honest: death is still a disturb-ing thought. How disturbing must it be for those who have no hope, who think that this life is all there is?

If this life is all there is, how far would you go to stay alive as long as possible? Would you eat well and exercise? That's okay. But . . . would you go so far as to kill others in order to stay alive longer? Would you take the life of someone else in order to make the time you have more enjoyable? That's a terrible thought, but it's happening in our nation today.

Abortion is just one example of committing mur-der to make your life more convenient. But there is another example. As I'm writing this just after Easter 2005, a woman named Terry Schiavo just died. I never met her, she lived thousands of miles away; but she was on the front page of the news for weeks before her death. Why? Because Terry Schiavo col-lapsed and suffered brain-damage several years ago, and since then was unable to do more than lie in a bed and communicate in very small ways. Although severely disabled, she was very much alive. However,

78

her husband argued that she wouldn't want to live that way. Through a series of prolonged court battles he won the right to withhold food and water from her. Less than two weeks later, Terry Schiavo died. She didn't die from her brain damage or other injuries. She died because she was purposely deprived of water and food. That's grotesque. What's even worse is that there are many, many people who will tell you it was the right thing to do. Sadly, while many will say this because they don't believe in Christ, many just say it because they haven't troubled themselves to think through the issues. You need to do better than that.

If this life is all there is, what do you do when death draws near? Do you continue living, even if it's painful or you resent how your movements are limited? Or do you decide to end your life when it's not going as you wish? Again, this is a real and present issue up for discussion, and a lot of the arguments are scary.

Get ready, because the debate over life and death is going to grow more heated and complex as you get older, so it's good for you to be prepared now. You'll be called upon to give intelligent answers about things like physician-assisted suicide, abortion, infanticide, euthanasia, and more. Then, just to drive you crazy, many of those who fight for these rights to die will maintain that war and the death penalty are wrong. So, before we get into the battle, it's good to survey the battlefield. Before we get to the questions and answers, we need to lay the foundation: we need to see what God says about life and death. So, here's what the witness of Scripture testifies to:

* **LIFE IS A GIFT FROM GOD.** As the Creator of the heavens and the earth (see Genesis 1 and 2), it is the Lord alone who gives life to all things (1 Timothy 6:13). Apart from Him, there is no life.

* **DEATH IS THE WAGES OF SIN** (Romans 6:23, 5:12). It was not part of God's plan for this creation. Rather He declares that death is an enemy (1 Corinthians 15:26), and He wants no one to die physically or spiritually (Ezekiel 18:32). Death is neither God's doing nor His gift. Therefore death is not a part of life—the two are complete opposites of one another.

80

* **GOD DESIRES THE DEATH OF NO ONE**, which is why He gave His Son Jesus Christ to die for the sins of the world, "that whoever believes in Him should not perish but have eternal life" (John 3:16; see also Romans 6:23). We already have eternal life in Christ by faith; while our bodies must still suffer physical death (unless Christ returns first), Jesus uses that last enemy (1 Corinthians 15:26) in order to be able to transform our bodies into sinless, eternal bodies once more (1 Corinthians 15:42–43). In heaven, entropy will no longer apply to us.

* **GOD KNOWS AND VALUES HUMAN LIFE FROM CONCEPTION.** As the book of Jeremiah begins, Jeremiah has been called to be a prophet, to speak God's Word at a time when nobody

wants to hear it. Jeremiah appears less than pleased with the prospect, so the Lord declares to Jeremiah, "Before I formed you in the womb I knew you, and before you were born I consecrated you; I appointed you a prophet to the nations" (Jeremiah 1:5). In Psalm 139, David declares, "For you formed my inward parts; you knitted me together in my mother's womb." In other words, God doesn't suddenly notice that we're here after we're born; as the Creator of heaven and earth, He is the one who personally creates you, though He uses your mom and dad as His means for doing so. At any rate, God recognizes you as a living human being from the moment you are conceived.

✱ THE VALUE THAT GOD PUTS ON YOU IS FAR GREATER THAN THE FACT THAT HE MADE YOU. God values you so much that He shed the blood of His only-begotten Son, sacrificing Him in order to give you life. St. Paul writes, "You are not your own, for you were bought with a price. So glorify God in your body" (1 Corinthians 6:19b–20). You have been redeemed, bought with the price of Jesus' own blood. That's how much God values you.

✱ HAVING CREATED US, GOD USES US AS HIS INSTRUMENTS TO SERVE HIM AND SERVE EACH OTHER (Luke 10:27). Way back in the Garden of Eden, He created Eve for Adam so that each of them would have someone to help and serve (Genesis 2:18). This call for serving remains today.

* **SOMETIMES, GOD USES US AS HIS ACTIVE INSTRUMENTS, WHERE WE SERVE BY DOING.** As Martin Luther explains in the meaning to the Fifth Commandment, "We should fear and love God so that we do not hurt or harm our neighbor in his body, but help and support him in every physical need" (*SC* p. 12). God is the One who ultimately defends the helpless (Psalm 10:14), He calls upon us especially to defend those who are weak and helpless; those who cannot speak for themselves: "Open your mouth for the speechless, in the cause of all who are appointed to die" (Proverbs 31:8 NKJV). We are called to "bear one another's burdens" (Galatians 6:2). Failure to do so is failing to keep the Law of Christ. Failing to help someone is a sin of omission, as mentioned in James 4:17, "So whoever knows the right thing to do and fails to do it, for him it is sin."

* **SOMETIMES, GOD USES US AS HIS PASSIVE INSTRUMENTS, WHERE WE SERVE BY BEING DONE TO—BY BEING SERVED.** For instance, a baby is an instrument of God by which He teaches parents how to serve day and night. When the baby's grown up, his parents might be crippled by age and disability; they'll be instruments of God by which He teaches to care for those in need and to honor life.

In a nutshell, that's what God says about life and death in His Word. As Christians, these are the doctrines we use in our decisions about life and death. These are your weapons for the battle.

To understand why the battle gets fought and what

strategies to use, let's take a moment and see what happens for those who deny God is the author and giver of life. Note how the first belief (denial of the one true, living God) may take people down different paths, but they'll still end up in the same place (man must take God's role), and that place leads to death.

Many today believe and practice that the Triune God is not the author and giver of life. This is because they believe that:

"There is no God (atheism), and we are simply an accident that happened."

"There is a god, but we can't possibly know what it is or if it has a plan for us" (agnosticism).

"There is a god, but not the God of Scripture. Therefore, we believe in a false god created by ourselves or another sinful person" (false religions).

"If there is no God, then there is no one greater than we who gives us value, who says we have worth."

"Since we can't know what that god out there somewhere says, we can't know what kind of worth it gives us."

"Since we make up who god is, we have to decide what sort of value it gives to us."

"Therefore, it's up to us to determine the value of us and the value of life. It means we get to be god! This means:"

"It's up to us to decide the value of life for ourselves. This means that it's up to me to determine how long I should live, and when my life isn't worth living anymore. If I don't like my quality of life or if I don't want to live this way, it means that I have the authority to take my life. It's up to us to decide the value of life for others who can't do it for themselves."

"It's up to us to decide when someone's life isn't worth living anymore. It's up to us to decide that their quality of life isn't good enough, or that they shouldn't have to live this way, or that death would be a better option than life."

SUICIDE: Killing oneself

PHYSICIAN-ASSISTED SUICIDE: Killing oneself with the help of a doctor

ABORTION: Killing of the unborn

INFANTICIDE: Killing of the recently born

EUTHANASIA: Killing of the disabled or elderly.

Do you see the progression there? The debate about life and death springs from one simple question: does God determine the value of human life, or do we? Those who believe God determines the value of human life oppose abortion, infanticide, euthanasia, and so forth. Those who believe man determines the value of human life will believe such practices are perfectly permissible. As a Christian, you must be aware of the big picture: these topics about the value of human life are directly connected to faith in the one true God.

Therefore, you need to keep a few things in mind when you debate these matters with others.

First, anyone who supports abortion or euthanasia can only do so if he rejects God's Word. As soon as you bring God into the argument, you'll be told that you can't do that because He doesn't exist, and that you're basing your arguments on religion, not fact. This is because he believes religion to be a matter of personal opinion, not truth. While you should still be ready to produce your defense from Scripture, it's also good to be equipped with arguments from science and common sense. We'll do that here.

Second, understand the rhetoric. Know words are used to make things sound better than they truly are. Those who oppose abortion are labeled "pro-life," but those who favor legalized-abortion are not labeled "pro-death" or even "pro-abortion." They define themselves as "pro-choice," which sounds a whole lot less bloodthirsty. Likewise, euthanasia is called "mercy-killing," as if deciding to take the life of the disabled or elderly is an act of kindness.

Third, understand that those who defend "pro-choice" and "mercy-killing" do not regard these terms as spin, or an attempt to make a sin sound better. Because they believe man bears the responsibility of deciding life and death, they believe abortion truly is a somber matter of choice and euthanasia is merciful.

The fourth and last thing to keep in mind is the

scariest of all. At the present time, the popular argument in our land is each individual should be able to determine when he or she dies. It is said this is an individual right. It's a personal freedom. However, this is already false: in the case of abortion, the child never gets the choice. In the case of Terry Schiavo whom I mentioned earlier, her husband decided, not her. Though so terribly hurt, she still possessed lungs that wanted to keep breathing, a heart which wanted to keep beating and a stomach which wanted to process food. Some would say this was involuntary, even a cruel thing for her body to do, and thus her husband did her a favor in fighting to end her life. From Scripture, you know her body continued to function because God designed her body for life, not death.

86

What do these examples teach us? They teach us, in this world, the one who has power makes the decision. Normally, the one who has power elects to sacrifice others so he can stay alive. Throughout history, there have been very few democracies: most kingdoms and nations have been ruled by one or by a very few. When a society leaves God and His Word behind, it is very possible the powerful few will decide who lives and who dies. It is very possible they will decide life on the basis of health or ability . . . or race . . . or religion. That's why World War II was fought. That's why nearly a million were slaughtered in Rwanda (1994), and why so many continue to die in Darfur. It could easily happen again. It will happen again. It is happening now.

But whatever the future holds for you, personally, or the world in general, you live with this certain promise: God values you so much that He has sacrificed His Son in order to save you from sin. The end of the story for you is eternal life. In the meantime, you live as one whose life is cherished by no less than God Himself.

Along the way, remember all of these questions of life all have to do with whether one believes in God as the giver of life.

Enough with the groundwork . . .

88

42. Where do babies come from?

Even though I always end up blushing and stammering when I answer this question, I promised at the start of this book to be honest and candid. So, here goes: when a man and a woman really love each other, they get married and place an order from the baby catalog. Whew, I'm blushing already. Seriously, I'm not opposed to discussing sex; but that really belongs in a second volume of this series called, *You Ask about Relationships*. For this volume, we should talk about when human life begins.

43. When does human life begin?

Thanks for asking, and right on cue. You would think that science has an answer for this question; but the truth is that it doesn't. Instead, you'll find a bunch of different theories. Some scientists argue that life begins at conception, because that's when the DNA gets mixed together from a sperm and an egg. Others say human life begins twelve days later because that's the last day twins might develop; by day thirteen you know how many persons are in there. Still others say human life begins when the baby can live independently of its mother. Usually, this means the baby has made it to 25 weeks after conception, because then its lungs are functioning and it can live if it's prematurely born. There's also the idea that a baby is human when it is conscious of its surroundings, when it can distinguish between itself and other things.

Now, let's run some of these through common sense. Start with the day-twelve argument: let's say you're walking toward a classroom door that's closed. You know there are people inside, but you don't know how many. Does this mean there are no humans in the room until you know how many there are? No. Likewise, whether it's going to be a single baby, twins, or octuplets, there's already human life in the womb before day twelve.

How about the suggestion the baby is human when it can live independently of its mother? I understand the importance of working lungs, but a baby can't live without a mother or caretaker for a looonnnggg time after it's born. Babies need to be fed, clothed. and sheltered; otherwise, they won't survive. So when does a baby really become independent of its mother?

Or consider the idea a baby is human when it can distinguish between itself and other things. I don't know about you, but I do my best to be unconscious of my surroundings for several hours each night. While I'm sleeping, do I cease to be human? Nope!

Remember, I love science; but once again, science doesn't have a definitive answer as to when life begins.

Common sense would, I think, argue that we're human from conception. From the moment that sperm meets egg, a human being is in development. It doesn't have all its parts yet, but you don't need all of your parts to be human—many people are walking around missing tonsils, a kidney, a spleen or a limb, but are no less human than they were before.

We have a better witness than common sense: we have God's Word. In Jeremiah 1:5, the Lord declares, "Before I formed you in the womb I knew you, and before you were born I consecrated you. . . ." As we stated earlier, the Word declares, from the very start at conception, a baby is known by God. Indeed, God is at work putting the child together. Therefore, it already has human life and value.

44. So does abortion take human life?

Yes, it does. It violates the Fifth Commandment, "You shall not murder" (Exodus 20:13). It fails to defend the helpless (Proverbs 31:8).

However, not everyone sees it this way; this is obvious, since abortion is legal in the United States and there are so many "pro-choice" voices out there. In speaking to pro-choice people, here's the tactic I use: I tell them all they have to do is prove to me the unborn baby isn't a human being, and I'll be pro-choice, too. Now, as we've seen above, scientists can't agree when life begins, so science doesn't officially know if an unborn baby is human or not. And if there's even a possibility the baby is human, shouldn't everybody do their best to protect this life?

91

You can try this argument, but I'm warning you: "pro-choice" advocates don't want to answer the question because they can't win. Instead of talking about human life, they'll talk about the importance of choice. You've probably heard the slogan, "A woman should have the right to choose [abortion]," or "A woman should have control over her own body." But no one has the right to end the life of the innocent, and the time for control comes about nine months before the baby is due, if you get my drift. Since a very small percentage of abortions take place because of rape or incest, self-control and abstinence would go a long way toward reducing the plague of abortion.

45. What about cases of rape and incest?

I really, really hate this question; but I'll go ahead and answer it. Before I do, let me be clear: rape and incest are two of the most devastating, cruel sins someone can inflict upon another. They shatter lives in ways which can never be recovered. Those who commit such crimes are the lowest of the low, and deserve serious prison time. Conversely, their victims deserve as much help as they can possibly receive.

But . . . does this make the baby any less of a human being?

And . . . if you have been hurt by someone, do you have the right to take the life of a third party? No. That's the thing: even if a baby is conceived in a violent crime, it's still a baby known by God and being formed by Him. It's still one for whom Christ died. I cannot possibly fathom the love necessary for the mother to carry this child to term; but I know it happens, and the Lord promises His all-sufficient grace.

46. What if it comes down to either the mother's life or the child's life?

Let's be clear: such cases make up a very small percentage of all abortions. In my opinion, those who use these mothers and children to defend legalized abortion deserve contempt. But since it does happen, here's the answer. In such a case, where either the mother or the child are going to die, then the mother and father are faced with a terrible choice—which life will they preserve? This will be one of the most gut-wrenching discussions known to man; and once the decision is made, they'll never be fully comforted they made the right choice. However, they can be completely certain and absolutely sure Christ died for mother, father, and child.

47. You said earlier those who are "pro-choice" have rejected the Word of God. Does this mean a person cannot be "pro-choice" and a Christian?

Unfortunately, you will find many churches and individuals who call themselves "Christian," who support legalized abortion. In such cases, examine what they teach about God's Word: I'm willing to bet they don't believe Scripture really is God's Word, and they openly admit it. If they have rejected the Word, they have rejected the Lord who gives it. They may call themselves Christians, but they are not.

However! All of us are sinful, and none of us has perfect understanding. It is possible there are some Christians who trust in Jesus as their Savior, yet believe the world's arguments about being "pro-choice." They have not consciously rejected the Word; they simply haven't thought it through, like you and I are doing here. For these brothers and sisters in Christ, we pray they would grow in faith, in the

93

knowledge of the Word, and appreciation for God's gift of life.

48. is it just me, or is it crazy that many favor the abortion of unborn children, but work very hard to save whales, seals and other animals? How does this work?

I think "crazy" is a pretty good description. Even though God made us stewards and calls for us to act responsibly and care for creation (see Question 38), I can't make any sense out of it.

Some people I have heard follow this rationale: a whale that has been born is a living creature whose life has begun, while an unborn baby is not a human being and has not begun to live. Some have gone so far as to argue the greatest danger to the earth is man, so man is more expendable than nature.

I'll tell you what I think, though this is only my best guess: in Romans 1, St. Paul describes what happens to those who reject the Lord and His Word, saying, "Claiming to be wise, they became fools, and exchanged the glory of the immortal God for images resembling mortal man and birds and animals and reptiles" (Romans 1:22–23). Those who support abortion on demand have rejected God as the one who gives life and value; instead, they take on the role of a god in deciding who lives or dies. Militant environmentalists reject God as the one who creates and preserves nature; in doing so, they glorify nature over the Lord. Both groups have a common bond: rebellion against the Lord. Sometimes people unite not because they have the same cause, but because they have the same enemy.

49. Can babies be saved before they're born?

More people may be asking this than you think. Besides the evil of intentional abortion, many children miscarry or die before birth. If your family hasn't been affected by this directly, it's only a matter of time until you know one who has. This is a bit of a tricky question, because unborn babies don't get a shot at the means of grace: Holy Absolution, Holy Baptism, and Holy Communion aren't available to them in the womb. (Some friends of mine will argue that the Word can reach unborn children, as their parents read them Bible stories or they hear the liturgy sung at church. I can't prove from Scripture they're wrong, but I can't prove they're right, either.) But here are some things we can be certain of.

> ✱ FIRST, the Lord knows the unborn and treasures them. He knew Jeremiah in the womb (Jeremiah 1:5), appointing him a prophet to the nations before Jeremiah could hear the Word or be circumcised. He knit David together (Psalm 139:13) and caused John the Baptist to leap in the

womb because Jesus was present there (Luke 1:41, 44). Why He permits some to miscarry, I do not know; but you can be sure that they are His creation.

✴ SECOND, the Lord doesn't bind Himself to His means of grace. He binds you and me to them. In other words, He tells you to run to His Word and His Sacraments for forgiveness, and nowhere else. But this doesn't mean He only works there; He can save babies in the womb, without the means of grace, if He desires.

✴ THIRD, the Lord hears and honors the prayers of parents on behalf of their children. He delivers their children apart from the children's faith, as in the case of Jairus (Mark 5:22–43) and the widow at Nain (Luke 7:11–17). I especially point out these because in those cases the Lord honored the prayers of the parents and raised up their children from death. Jesus' death on the cross was as much for parents today as for them; therefore, for the sake of Jesus, God honors parents' prayers today no less than those of old.

So, yes! Babies can be saved before they're born. This is in the hands of God.

50. What are stem cells?

When a human body starts developing inside a mother's womb, it doesn't start out with heart cells, lung cells, liver cells and the like. After all, it starts out as only one cell when sperm and egg get together. Somehow, it needs to develop all those different organs—this is what stem cells do. Stem cells are cells which can turn into all sorts of different body parts. (An evolutionist may point to this as proof that God is not necessary, but doesn't this further prove how creative and awesome God is?) Doctors really like researching this, because they think they can learn to make stem cells grow into replacement body parts for people who are sick. Let's say I need a new pancreas; stem cell research offers the possibility doctors could grow me a new one.

51. What's the controversy with stem cells?

The controversy is many scientists prefer to conduct research with stem cells from human embryos, which is what unborn babies are called until they've been in the womb for eight weeks. (After conception, babies go through different stages as they develop, and are called different things. A baby is first a zygote, then a morula, then a blastocyst, then an embryo, and then a fetus. When speaking of the unborn children, I always use the terms "baby" or "child" or "little one." Calling an unborn child a

97

"blastocyst" or a "fetus" makes it easier to think of him or her as less than a human being. That makes it seem more okay to dispose of these kids, and I'm not going to play that game.) When these stem cells are "harvested," it means the death of the embryo—it means killing a human being. This violates the Fifth Commandment, taking a life rather than defending the helpless. While I wouldn't mind getting a new pancreas if I needed one, it can't be at the expense of somebody else's life—especially the life of a helpless, unborn child.

On the bright side, scientists report they may be able to use stem cells from umbilical cords, and maybe even adult fat cells. Now, here's a supply that (a) people don't mind losing and (b) isn't going to run out anytime soon. (I might just go have a double bacon cheeseburger for the cause of science!) At present, adult stem cells aren't as versatile for scientists as embryonic stem cells; however, they can be used without the death of the unborn.

52. What is cloning?

Cloning is the act of taking a living being's genetic material and creating a duplicate. Scientists have, for instance, cloned sheep, frogs and other animals. There's been talk of cloning human beings for one reason or another, and South Korean scientists claimed to do so in 2004. Instead of a new human being made out of the DNA of a mom and dad, the new human being is an identical twin of one or the other, nothing more.

53. Does the Bible address cloning?

Not directly, but I think this is the verse to keep in mind, "And God blessed [Adam and Eve]. And God said to them, 'Be fruitful and multiply and fill the earth and subdue it and have dominion over the fish of the sea and over the birds of the heavens and over every living thing that moves on the earth'" (Genesis 1:28).

As we said earlier, God is the author and creator of life; in His design, He creates life by use of a mom and a dad. God uses people as His instruments, but He's the creator. Cloning attempts to create life outside of God's ways and means. (It doesn't create life, anyway, but only copies what's there.) While man can clone, the Lord never said we should. Cloning is an attempt by man to take over the role of God.

We're not talking about changing a cookie recipe here. This is about human life; we do well to recognize God alone as the creator.

54. What is euthanasia?

Euthanasia is the practice of ending the life of one who is sick, elderly, or disabled. It's from a Greek word that means "good death," and is sometimes referred to as "mercy-killing." Euthanasia advocates try to dress it up in better clothes by calling it "death with dignity." It can be done actively, by injecting an overdose of anesthetic into the victim, or passively, by withholding food and water. When euthanasia is

99

committed with the help of a doctor at the request of the patient, it's called "physician-assisted suicide."

55. is euthanasia murder?

Yes! This violates the Fifth Commandment, "You shall not murder" (Exodus 20:13). Remember, God calls us to defend the helpless (Proverbs 31:8), not to hasten their death.

56. How should we treat those who are severely disabled or dying?

We should treat them as those whom God knows and values. We should treat them as people for whom Christ died in order to give them life. We should treat them as instruments whom God is still using for His purposes, because they are all of these things—and no less than we are.

And back up a minute from the cross. On His way to His death on the cross for us, how did Jesus treat those who were sick, outcast and dying? He healed them, restored them and delivered them. He didn't shun them or suggest they were better off dead. Now, obviously, we can't miraculously heal people as He did, but we certainly are not to take away life that He has given. Instead, we should endeavor to help others as much as we can.

57. Sometimes, people argue for euthanasia by pointing to someone who is severely disabled or paralyzed and saying, "Would you want to live this way?" How do you answer?

I would answer, "No! I wouldn't want to live that way." To be perfectly honest, I'm quite the chicken and the thought of living that way scares me. But here's the real question: is this my choice to make? Is it man's decision? No! We are the Lord's, and the Lord will use us as His instruments. He does not abandon us, but remains faithful. He further promises that He provides sufficient grace to keep us faithful in suffering. Even better, we have the Lord's promise that the suffering is not the end: "For I consider that the sufferings of this present time are not worthy to be compared with the glory which shall be revealed in us" (Romans 8:18). St. Paul doesn't write these words to trivialize the suffering, but to make known how glorious the eternal life is which awaits us for the sake of Christ.

58. is there a time when it's okay to stop a treatment for someone who is dying?

There are a few. For instance, one is when the treatment isn't doing anything, and this happens as a body gets sicker. Obviously, if the treatment isn't

101

doing anything, there's no reason to keep doing it.

Such decisions will vary greatly in every case, so I'm not real keen on addressing them here, because each case is so different and there's not enough room in this book for a good discussion. When such things happen, it's best to make these decisions with a doctor and pastor who both value God's gift of life.

But this, I think, is important: when considering these things, the Christian does not approach these questions asking, "When is my life no longer worth living?" The Christian approaches these decisions asking things like, "My life is not my own, for I have been bought with a price. Does this decision honor God and His gift of life?"

(By the way, if your family has been involved in decisions like these, you already know that they're horrible. They can't be any other way. Even if people make all the right decisions, they'll always second-guess themselves. They may even know they made the wrong decision. That's why it's so important to remember, when all is said and done, we are saved by our Savior's death and resurrection—not by how well we make decisions under stress.)

59. i heard somebody say withholding food and water from a dying patient who can't feed himself isn't the same as starving them. is this true?

No, and you can use your common sense for this

question. Imagine a mother making this argument about her newborn child, "I'm not starving him by not feeding him, because he can't do it himself." The mother would be arrested pretty quickly for endangering her child—perhaps even attempted murder. (Recently nearby, a woman was arrested for treating horses that way!) It's a sin of omission, of failing to care for someone in need. Why is withholding food from someone who's dying any less of a sin?

60. So if Christians are so concerned with preserving, defending and honoring life, how come so many Christians support the death penalty?

103

Here's a quick quiz question: Who can make an exception to a law of God?

Answer: God can. In this case, He does—in Romans 13:

> For rulers are not a terror to good conduct, but to bad. Would you have no fear of the one who is in authority? Then do what is good, and you will receive his approval, for he is God's servant for your good. But if you do wrong, be afraid, for he does not bear the sword in vain. For he is the servant of God, an avenger who carries out God's wrath on the wrongdoer. **(Romans 13:3–4)**

Note that rulers—governments, are supposed to

be a terror to bad guys. As part of punishing evildoers, rulers are allowed to "bear the sword." Swords
aren't used to nudge or poke; they're used to do
things like stab, smite, slay, separate limb from limb.
Stuff like that.

So rulers have the right to punish evildoers, in
order to discourage crime and to protect the innocent.
This punishment can include the death penalty.

61. Do governments have to have the death penalty?

No. Romans 13 gives them a right, but not a
requirement.

62. According to the Bible, for what crimes should the death penalty be used?

Back in the Old Testament, the Lord required the
death penalty for several crimes, including worshiping false gods (Leviticus 20:2); blaspheming God's
name (Leviticus 24:16); cursing your father or mother (Leviticus 20:9); adultery (Leviticus 20:10); murder (Numbers 35:17); and even gathering sticks on
the Sabbath (Numbers 15:35).

This means one of two things: either our nation
has completely failed at punishing stick-gatherers, or
else it's time for a Levitical Law Alert.

You guessed right. It's time for a Levitical Law

Alert. If you haven't read Question 17 on which laws in the Bible still apply, go back and do that now.

Now!

If you've already read Question 17, then you're coolly saying, "These are all examples of levitical law, and so they don't apply to us anymore." You're quite right. So for what crimes does the Bible still require the death penalty?

The New Testament doesn't give us a list, nor does it make this the responsibility of priests. It leaves this in the hands of rulers and governments. Some governments abolish the death penalty, while others retain it.

63. Since rulers have the right to use the death penalty, do they have the right to execute anyone they want?

105

No. Rulers are given the right to bear the sword in order to discourage evil. When a ruler puts people to death for reasons other than protecting the innocent from the evil, he is misusing his authority and committing the sin of murder. Tragically in our world today, governments will execute people for "crimes" that aren't crimes at all—like having a different opinion. Or being a Christian. Despite the pressures on the Church in America today, we have it easy; a lot of our brothers and sisters in Christ risk their lives daily to bear His name.

That's also why it's important for us to pray daily for our rulers, that they might be wise and just (1 Timothy 2:1–2).

64. Doesn't the death penalty risk putting an innocent man or woman to death?

Yes. That's why it should only be used with utmost care. Even then, some who are innocent will lose their lives, so rulers and nations must decide whether or not the risk is worth the danger.

To be honest, this line of thought always leads me to a reason for thanks to God. One of the tougher bits about living in this world is some people are going to like me and some people aren't. Some might be able to give a good reason, while a few have tried to hurt me for no good reason. But no matter how man judges me or misjudges me, it's the Lord who gives the final verdict on the Last Day. He'll declare me innocent, forgiven, for Jesus' sake. In fact, He already does.

While execution ends a life in this world, it is not the end. The repentant Christian who is wrongly put to death has eternal life; so does the repentant Christian who mistakenly executed an innocent man.

65. So if i come across a bad guy, can i whack him as a service to my community?

Not unless you're authorized by the government of the community. God gives the right to bear the sword to rulers, not to everyone. When someone else starts taking out the bad guys on his own, he's called a vigilante.

Here's how it works in the beautiful state of Idaho, where I live. The top ruler in the state is the governor, given the right to bear the sword. However, the governor's got a few things to do, so the law says each county is to have a sheriff and each city can have a police force. These officers, as part of government, have the right to track down the bad guys—with deadly force if necessary. Since that's not my job (my vocation, my calling from God), I don't have the mission to go track down outlaws and ne'er-do-wells.

However, the government of Idaho also gives me the right of self-defense. In certain situations, where I believe that my life is in danger, I have the right to defend myself with deadly force. If I do this, I'm not a vigilante. I'm bearing the sword because the government said I could.

So heed this warning well—don't come breaking into my house in the middle of the night—I know Kung Pao.

66. Do rulers have permission to wage wars?

Yes, because this is part of bearing the sword (Romans 13:3–4).

67. Is war a good thing?

No, I'd call it more of a tragic necessity in this

world. First, let's be clear. War is an ugly thing. It's the ultimate breakdown in society where two sides have stopped talking and have decided to kill each other instead. Those who fight on the front lines, or those who are innocently caught in the battle, witness and suffer a horror that most of us can't imagine. So, as Martin Luther said, war is a plague—but it prevents a greater plague from happening. Let's plug in some common sense and look at history. Would the world be better off without the horror of World War II, but instead with all of Europe controlled by Nazi Germany? Hardly! Because nations try to expand their power at the expense of others, war is a brutal necessity to prevent the spread of evil and violence.

68. May governments wage wars for any reason?

No. Beyond giving rulers the right to bear the sword in Romans 13, the Bible says little about war. However, back in the 4th century, a Christian named Augustine proposed the "Just War" theory, which is still recognized today. Augustine's thoughts on this go on for quite a while, so let's boil it down to two points for our discussion.

> **FIRST**, it's only a just war if it has proper authority. If a legitimate ruler declares war against another nation, that's proper authority because he has the right to bear the sword. If I declare war against another coun-

try—even if I have a good reason and some troops to back it up—it's not a just war because I'm not a ruler.

SECOND, it's a just war if you didn't start it. That's really simplistic, but think about it for a second. The one who starts the war is the aggressor, the one who wants to attack and kill to take something that isn't his. Therefore, the one who fights back is defending—and rulers bear the sword in order to protect their citizens from evil. So, a ruler may fight a just war in order to defend his own nation; or, if he's called upon by another ruler to defend that nation, he may do that, too.

In other words, rulers are to obey the Fifth Commandment, too. While they must bear the sword to punish evildoers, they should also help and support their neighbor in every physical need.

69. So since a just war is possible, are you saying wars are fought with pure motives?

No! Honestly, sin clings to everything we do. While a nation may fight in a war where the primary reason is just, there's a good chance there will be ulterior motives, excessive violence, unnecessary death, and more. When people are trying to kill each other, there's not going to be much purity of anything. War is a messy business.

70. May a nation attack on foreign soil to prevent an attack on the homeland?

If a "just war" is one you don't start, some might argue you can't launch a preemptive strike to prevent an attack: the other guy has to shoot first. So, imagine (as if this takes much imagination these days) that a rogue leader with a violent history gets a nuclear missile and has it aimed at a large American city, ready to go. Some may argue you have to wait until the missile launches, or else you've started the fight. Others will say the fight was already started when the bad guy got the missile, since everyone knows that he's going to use it to hurt people, and he needs to be stopped.

In this case, I go back to the Small Catechism and the explanation to the Fifth Commandment, "You shall not murder." Keeping this command means both that you don't hurt your neighbor, and that you prevent harm from coming to him. The Seventh Commandment demands that we protect our neighbor's property and business. Therefore, if my neighbor and his goods are about to be vaporized and I'm the proper authority, I have the responsibility to prevent it. So—and there will be debate on this—it's my opinion that a nation may launch a preemptive strike (even an invasion) if there is a clear and imminent threat against it.

Here's the disclaimer and the problem: what makes for a "clear threat"? May a nation attack because of a rumor? How solid must the evidence be? If there's a 99% chance that the threat is real, there seems to be a good case for crushing it. But what about a 90% chance? A 75% chance? Furthermore, what makes for an "imminent threat"? Does the enemy have to be ready to inflict damage the same day? Within two weeks? Within the next six months? What if there's only a really good potential the enemy is going to do something in the future? What if it's not a nuclear missile, but the possibility of an attack on an embassy?

Do you see the challenge? Where do you draw the line and launch the attack? This is one more reason why I don't want to be the president. It's another reason to follow our Lord's bidding and pray for our rulers (1 Timothy 2:1–2).

71. May a Christian be a soldier?

Yes, and we have some good Scriptural evidence for this. When John the Baptist was preaching in the wilderness by the Jordan River, all sorts of people came out to hear him. All sorts of people were convicted of their sins and repented. All sorts of people wanted to know what they should be doing to amend their sinful lives. Among them were soldiers, who asked John the Baptist, "And we, what shall we do?" Look carefully at John's answer: "Do not extort money from anyone by threats or by false accusation, and be content with your wages" (Luke 3:14). Did John tell them to go A.W.O.L., to repent of being soldiers and find an honest job instead? Nope. He told them to be soldiers—good soldiers who didn't threaten people or take things. He said they could remain in the military and still be saved.

72. But can a Christian soldier kill without sinning?

It sounds strange, but here it is: as a person, the Christian is to obey the Fifth Commandment, "You shall not murder." As a soldier, the Christian bears the sword on behalf of the ruler. Therefore, in the middle of battle, a Christian soldier may kill with a clear conscience, because he's supposed to! That's what God has given him to do according to his vocation.

This assumes that the Christian is following "just orders" (which is far different from "just following orders") and fighting in a just war.

Now, having said this, a lot of Christians return from battle with all sorts of guilt, doubt, and questions. A soldier might feel terribly guilty even if his fighting was courageous and right. After heavy fighting, he may find it difficult to sort out what is sinful and what is not in war. He may well have fired a shot and killed where, had he had more time to evaluate, he might have held fire and spared a life. There's not much time for decisions in the middle of battle.

Because of this, it's so important for soldiers to remember: heaven is not theirs because of their perfect battle skills. Heaven is theirs because Christ died to save them, to forgive them for all of their sins. That's true for everyone—not just soldiers; but those who have seen action understand life and death far better than the rest of us.

73. Can someone who commits suicide still go to heaven?

Before you read this answer, make sure you've read the introductory stuff to this section. Please.

Among other things, the introductory notes demonstrated that you're no accident, but created by God. He has given you your physical life. He places such a value upon you that He's given His Son on the cross to redeem you. He desires to use you as His instrument of service in this world. You are God's beloved child, and He has given you life, hope, and purpose.

In terms of religion, then, suicide is a declaration that one wants nothing to do with God and His gifts. Although it is often described as "taking one's own life," it is really "rejecting the life that God has given." Those who reject life also reject God's desire to use them as His instruments.

We haven't even mentioned, yet, about the pain that is sinfully inflicted by those who commit suicide upon those who love them. Suicide is a horrible, evil thing.

So maybe you've heard, as I was taught, that it's impossible for someone who has committed suicide to be saved. But I don't believe this to be completely the case.

The Bible says that the only unforgivable sin is unbelief (see, for instance, Mark 16:16), a rejection of Jesus and His forgiveness. It also declares that we are forgiven for the sins we don't realize (Psalm 19:12). Is it possible that a distressed Christian can commit suicide in a crazed moment of despair, rather than an intentional rejection of God's gifts? Is it possible for one to repent during suicide, but too late to prevent death? I do believe it's possible. The door's not quite shut. But one can never be certain.

At all times, remember God's love for you—your life is not your own—you have been bought with the price of Christ's own blood.

As a pastor, I don't really want to deal with this too much in general here, because there are too many questions. This is a matter best left to individual situations, as you can see by the next question.

74. What about a soldier who throws himself on a grenade during battle to save his comrades? is that suicide?

Not everyone who chooses to die is guilty of suicide: some are to be praised for their sacrifice instead. The soldier who sacrifices himself to save others does an honorable thing, as does the citizen who dies while saving a child from fire or drowning. Jesus declared, "Greater love has no one than this, that someone lays down his life for his friends" (John 15:13). He then went to the cross and did exactly that, dying for the sins of the world.

Now, just in case you think it's always easy to distinguish between suicide and sacrifice, let me give you a couple of examples to think about. Soldiers may suffer from battle fatigue to the point that they simply don't want to live if they have to stay on the front line. So let's say such a soldier throws himself on the grenade: did he do this because he wanted to save his friends, or end his life and misery in the trenches?

The other example is a painful news story from a while back. A young boy heard his parents worrying that they didn't have enough money for groceries, so he took his own life in the backyard. His awkward note indicated he simply, and without guile, wanted to help his parents save money by reducing the amount of food they needed to buy. His death was ruled a suicide, yet he believed he was making a sacrifice.

Would you care to judge either heart? I would not. Instead, I'd rather commend each one to the Lord's mercy, and continue to rejoice that the Lord has not forsaken a world so messed up by sin as this one.

This is, after all, a dying world. It's not just the Second Law of Thermodynamics (entropy, the law that everything falls apart); no, it's the wages of sin (Romans 6:23). The very fact people view death as a friend and helper (abortion, euthanasia, etc.) only shows how deceptive and deep sin is. In the midst of all this, Christians look a little crazy for insisting that life, no matter how helpless or injured, is a gift to be preserved.

I spend a lot of time visiting the sick and the dying; and frankly, I'd be very depressed were it not for the Gospel. Even though this world is passing away, it is not a God-forsaken world. Jesus continues to visit His people with forgiveness and life. This world is not the end. Jesus died and rose again. He will raise His people up to everlasting life.

Read this introduction
to make sure you're
not part of the problem.

118 Section Four: Church & State

It was not George Santayana who said, "Those who never change their socks are condemned to dine alone," though whoever said it has a really good point. Santayana did say, "Those who cannot remember the past are condemned to repeat it." He was absolutely right. I get a bit grumpy when I hear so many people debate church-state issues when it's obvious they haven't done their history. That's the point of this introductory section before we move on to the questions.

Some of the questions in this book might seem far away from your life: instead of "You ask," more like "Who asked?" But here's a section of questions which involve you more than you might think, because you're on the front lines of the battle. You see, when it comes to figuring out the relationship between church and state, between secular government and religion, most of the landmark lawsuits and court decisions have come out of schools. For instance:

* Should there be prayer in public schools?

* Can a public school bus take students to a Christian school?

* May a teacher read a Bible verse out loud in class?

* May a student group have a Bible study in a public school classroom?

119

An awful lot of the law about church and state today comes from the classroom. You're in the middle of the fight, those laws shape the education you receive. That education is shaping you, which is all the more reason to know what's going on.

We can add other big questions from other parts of

society, like:

* May a courtroom have a display of the Ten Commandments on the wall?

* May City Hall have a nativity scene at Christmas? What about a Christmas tree?

Be prepared, because the answers aren't as easy as you think. They're almost always frustrating because they're never clear-cut or consistent, and you'll see why by the end of this section. Furthermore, it's only going to get more confusing in your lifetime. One of the reasons why it's so confusing is so many people don't care about history; if you don't care about history, you're going to be part of the problem because you have amnesia. So, once again, read the introductory stuff first to build the foundation. After that, the questions and answers will make a whole lot more sense.

We've been using science as one of our witnesses throughout the book. For looking at church and state, our big witness is going to be the social science of history. Only by knowing what has happened will you understand what's going on today . . . and what may happen tomorrow.

Two Kingdoms

Before we look at how church and state interact, we'd better figure out what they are and what they're for. This is important, because as a Christian you're part of both. In fact, both church and state are ordained by God for your good, though with very different purposes.

We find the purpose of government in Romans 13:

> Let every person be subject to the governing authorities. For there is no authority except from God, and those that exist have been instituted by God. Therefore whoever resists the authorities resists what God has appointed, and those who resist will incur judgment. For rulers are not a terror to good conduct, but to bad. Would you have no fear of the one who is in authority? Then do what is good, and you will receive his approval, for he is God's servant for your good. But if you do wrong, be afraid, for he does not bear the sword in vain. For he is the servant of God, an avenger who carries out God's wrath on the wrongdoer. Therefore one must be in subjection, not only to avoid God's wrath but also for the sake of conscience. For the same reason you also pay taxes, for the authorities are ministers of God, attending to this very thing. Pay to all what is owed to them: taxes to whom taxes are owed, revenue to whom revenue is owed, respect to whom respect is owed, honor to

whom honor is owed.
(Romans 13:1–7)

There you go. The state is established by God in order to enforce good laws, protect citizens, preserve order, and punish evildoers. This is primarily to help the Church in its mission (1 Timothy 2:2).

The purpose, or mission, of the Church is summed up well in Matthew 28:

> And Jesus came and said to them,
> "All authority in heaven and on earth
> has been given to Me. Go therefore
> and make disciples of all nations, bap-
> tizing them in the name of the Father
> and of the Son and of the Holy Spirit,
> teaching them to observe all that I
> have commanded you. And behold,
> I am with you always, to the end of
> the age." **(Matthew 28:18–20)**

After He arose from the dead the Lord Jesus commanded His disciples to baptize and teach His Word to all nations. He commanded them to spread the Gospel. This is the mission of the Church until He returns in glory.

Different missions require different tools. To protect citizens, God gives secular government the right to bear the sword: the state may arrest, imprison, and even execute evildoers for the sake of society. It may also wage just wars against aggressive enemy nations. (See Romans 13 above, as well as Questions 66–70 in the "Life and Death" section of this book.) The secular government may exercise mercy, but it is not about grace and forgiveness. In contrast, to give out the forgiveness of sins, God gives the Church the "sword of the Spirit"—the Word of God. He gives the Church His Word to proclaim and His Sacraments to administer. That is how sins are forgiven, and how disciples are made. The Church is not given the right to exercise temporal power—it is not to exercise the sword, imprison or execute unbelievers, or declare war.

Different missions have different organizations. In secular kingdoms, people have different ranks and levels of authority. There are rulers who rule and subjects who obey. All must respect the authorities that God places in power. (This is true for all sorts of "governments" in your life. At your summer job, your

123

	CHURCH	STATE
MISSION	Proclaim the Gospel, give out forgiveness	Enforce laws and preserve order
INSTRUMENTS	Word and Sacrament	Sword and force
ORGANIZATION	All equally sinful and redeemed	Different ranks and levels of authority

boss has authority, and you have the privilege of doing what he says.) In the spiritual kingdom, all are equal before God (Galatians 3:28)—equally sinful and equally redeemed. This is not a place for partiality or rank (James 2), so Christians live by serving one another—not ordering one another around.

This means that you and I live in two very different kingdoms with different missions, tools and structures. That's okay, because that's exactly how God intended it to be. Believe it or not, it was no different for Jesus as He prepared for His crucifixion. Standing before Pilate, He said, "My kingdom is not of this world. If My kingdom were of this world, My servants would have been fighting, that I might not be delivered over to the Jews. But My kingdom is not from the world" (John 18:36). As He spoke, the eternal King of kings also submitted to the authority of Pilate, even when Pilate declared Him innocent (three times!) and then sentenced Him to be scourged and crucified. It is an amazing, profound truth; the Son of God considered Himself a citizen under human authority. The Lord thus made clear Christians are also members of the State; they are citizens of a nation on earth, and subject to both Him and their earthly rulers.

However, the fact that Pilate sentenced Jesus to be crucified also demonstrates the two kingdoms can clash pretty violently. How can they coexist? From the witnesses of history and common sense, there are really four options. If you don't like history, you'll be tempted to skip the next few paragraphs; but the whole church-state debate will make a lot more sense if you keep reading.

The Three Options That the Founding Fathers Learned by Staying Awake in History Class

option one: isolation

Some religious scholars have taught you can be a member of God's kingdom or an earthly nation—but not both. Some have withdrawn to a lonely compound, while others have taught that believers should avoid involvement in society as much as possible. They shouldn't own property, vote, take oaths, run for office, or serve in the military. This doesn't work: instead, it thwarts the mission of both state and the Church. Christians are to submit to governing authorities, not avoid them. Furthermore, how can they make disciples of all nations if they're avoiding all nations?

option two: the church runs the state.

This was the option of the Middle Ages. In medieval times, the Roman Catholic Church appoint-

125

ed rulers, set prices, and waged wars. It sounds good in theory, but it's not a good idea at all. If you give an electrician's tools to a plumber, he can't do either job well. When the Roman Catholic Church took over the tools of secular government, it nearly stopped being the Church. Rather than make disciples of all nations by Word and Sacrament, it used the sword and force. The Gospel was nearly lost, and the Church nearly disappeared. Christians who sought to proclaim the true Gospel were persecuted. Whenever the Church has gotten secular power in history, it has hurt the preaching of the Gospel.

option three: the state runs the church.

Following the Reformation to provide structure and help for the new Lutheran Church, Luther asked the German princes to step in. This led to the European tradition of the government running the Church. But this is bad, too. Secular governments aren't interested in making disciples and preaching the Gospel; therefore, when given control of the Church, they seek to reshape it into a tool that helps govern. The Church is remodeled so that it's not about Jesus and forgiveness, but about creating harmony among citizens and strengthening the state. Historically, when the government controls the Church, the Church ceases to proclaim Christ.

the fourth option
and the first amendment

Now, the Founding Fathers of the United States knew their history, and they didn't like any of the options above. They also knew the thirteen colonies pretty well. Many of these colonies were founded by people who left Europe to practice their religion freely. There was no way they would sign on to a constitution allowing rulers to control their religion, or one allowing one church to control the government. They'd left Europe to avoid these things. On the other hand, many colonists wanted to make sure their beliefs had authority in their own colony. So the Founding Fathers came up with option four—coexistence. This is the great experiment known as the First Amendment to the Constitution, which started with these words: "Congress shall make no law respecting an establishment of religion, or prohibiting the free exercise thereof. . . ."

What did this mean? It meant that the United States government couldn't establish a state religion. It could never say, "From henceforth, this nation will be Roman Catholic," or "Lutheran," or "Navel-Gazers." The federal government couldn't give special treatment to one religion or denomination over another.

However—and these are big "howevers" that most people don't seem to know:

> *This didn't mean that church and
> state were totally separate! The feder-

al government could give money to various religious groups, as long as it didn't show preference to one religion over another. So, for instance, President Thomas Jefferson gave taxpayer dollars to Roman Catholic priests for their work among the Indians, including the spread of the Gospel; this was okay, as long as Puritans and Baptists could also receive funds.

*While the First Amendment guaranteed that the United States would not have an official national religion, individual states still could. Maryland could be a Roman Catholic state, while Connecticut could be Puritan. The state of Massachusetts had a state church until 1833!

Your state could have been a Lutheran paradise! But, alas, a couple of little things happened, like a war and a school bus ride.

1 + 14 = Separation

The first thing that happened was the Civil War. Imagine for a moment that you're living in Georgia in 1861. You go to bed one night as an American citizen. You wake up the next morning to find out that Georgia has seceded and is no longer part of the United States. Because you're in Georgia, you're no longer a U. S. citizen. Your state has robbed you of your United States citizenship and rights, and made you a citizen of a different country.

Hey! Can they do that?

They could in 1861; so after the Civil War in 1868, Congress added the Fourteenth Amendment to the Constitution. Among other things, the Fourteenth Amendment said that a state couldn't make a law that contradicted federal law. If a state makes a law that does so, you have the right to appeal to the Federal Government. This is, for the most part, a good thing: if your state tries to secede and declare you are no longer an American citizen, you could file a lawsuit and the Federal Government would put an end to this practice.

The second thing which happened was the school bus system in Ewing, New Jersey, in 1947. The township contained public schools and a bunch of Roman Catholic parochial schools. The local Board of Education reasoned:

✱ Our job is to make sure the kids around here get an education.

✱ Roman Catholic schools educate a lot of the kids around here, and really help us out by keeping our public classrooms from being too crowded.

✱ Therefore, let's help the Roman Catholic schools help us by using our school buses to get their student to school and back.

Makes sense to me.

But it didn't fly with a local taxpayer named Everson, who filed a lawsuit. Everson argued:

* The First Amendment says that the United States can't force me to support a religion with my tax dollars. Therefore, the U.S. could never force me to help pay for busing for Roman Catholic Students.

* The Fourteenth Amendment says that the State of New Jersey can't make a law which contradicts federal law.

* Therefore, neither the State of New Jersey nor any of its local governments can force me to help pay for busing for Roman Catholic students.

The case went to the United States Supreme Court, and Everson won 5-4. The rumor that the justices played "rock-paper-scissors" to decide are unfounded, especially since I just started it here. But before you groan or grumble, there was good news and bad news in the decision.

The good news is that the Supreme Court repeated that the government couldn't force anyone to participate in a religion: the state had no business telling you what you should believe or not believe. This is very, very good.

The bad news is that the Supreme Court went further, arguing that government and religious groups couldn't interact at all. There was to be a "wall of separation between church and state." Therefore, for instance, even if a Lutheran School is doing a city a big favor by educating half of the students in the community, the government can't give assistance to the school.

Lots of lawsuits followed the Everson case. Some argued that Everson went too far, while others argued it didn't go far enough. Ever since, pretty much every court decision has stuck with Everson, declaring government has no place in religion and religion has no place in government. Ideally, according to the courts, the two should have nothing to do with each other.

(By the way, this is why evolution gets the advantage in the public school system. Everybody knows part of studying this world is knowing where it came from; but since you can't talk about God in school, you have to have some sort of theory—no matter how stinky—to explain the origin of everything. In my opinion, evolution is popular not because it's solid, but because it's a convenient way to talk about the origin of the world without mentioning God.)

131

I've got four things left to say.

First, you already know that it's impossible for church and state to have nothing to do with each other. You're a citizen of a nation and a Christian who belongs to the Kingdom of God. Unless you figure out how to have nothing to do with yourself, then your citizenship and your Christianity must have something to do with each other. That's true on every level, up through the Federal Government. This will be clear in the questions that follow.

Second: note how things evolved throughout history. The First Amendment of the Bill of Rights said that the Federal Government couldn't show preference to a certain religion or interfere with personal religious beliefs, but it could support activities by religious groups. The Fourteenth Amendment said the same applied to state and local governments. The Everson decision determined the First and Fourteenth Amendments really meant that no level of government could interact with religion whatsoever. Where will it go from here?

Third, and this may surprise you: I really don't blame the courts for their decision in the Everson case. While it creates a lot of problems, I can at least sympathize with what they did. Here's why. When the Founding Fathers wrote the First Amendment, just about the only religious groups to be found in America were under the umbrella of Christianity. There were Roman Catholics, Congregationalists, Baptists, and Puritans, all of whom took their doctrine seriously and didn't especially like each other very much. The purpose of the First Amendment was primarily to keep one Christian group from persecuting another Christian group. It was much simpler back then to ensure each religious group received equal help and recognition from the government. Today, the religious groups in America are nearly too many to count: you have Christians, Muslims, Mormons, Buddhists, Hindus, Jehovah's Witnesses, Eckankar, Bahai, and a bunch of other organized religions, not to mention the guy down the street who's started his own church because he thinks God talks directly to him. If I were a court justice in charge of making sure that every religious group got equal treatment from the government, I think I'd probably say, "The only way to make sure that government helps all these people equally is if the government helps none of them. That's equal treatment." For the time being, anyway, you can expect that our nation's courts will pretty much always decide that religion doesn't belong in public life. This view is called secularism.

Fourth, when you're answering questions about church and state, you have to understand that secularism is only half of the story. If only it were so easy.

the other half of the story: multiculturalism

The other half of the story takes less time to describe, but it's a much more annoying problem called multiculturalism. The United States is a nation full of people from many different nations and cul-

133

tures. This is a good thing, it's important people respect one another. However, multiculturalism can go crazy and insist that we not only respect other cultures, but accept all practices as equally good. Therefore, for example, a culture where women are treated as slaves and beaten by their husbands is just as good as a culture where women are respected as equals in society. You're not allowed to criticize other cultures, because that's how people supposedly want to live.

As a Christian, you can see the problem with this philosophy. It's built on man, not God. It's built on the idea that however man decides to live must be good, because man's in charge of deciding how to live. It rejects the idea that God gives His Law to tell us how to treat each other.

134

Now, multiculturalism is a big part of public school education. Students are routinely taught all about other cultures and societies, which is not necessarily a bad thing.

It's also true that different people living in different cultures create different religions. You cannot completely understand their culture without studying their religion. You cannot understand the Middle East without studying Islam. You cannot understand India without studying Hinduism. The religions are part of the culture, how people live their lives every day. Therefore, multiculturalism says, as part of studying culture in public schools, students have to study religion. Again, that makes sense.

But here's the problem: the playing field isn't

level. Multiculturalism insists it's okay to study just about any religion in public school except Christianity. Why? Because Christianity has spread around the world, so it's not a religion that goes with one culture. It's found in cultures all over the world; and because it's found in nearly all cultures, it's not considered to be part of any one culture.

That seems to be the reason why students may study all sorts of religions in school, but they can't talk about Christianity. One example took place in California in 2002, where many public schools featured a unit on Islam. Students were required to learn Muslim teachings, memorize verses from the Koran, wear a robe, and adopt an Islamic name. School officials argued that this was not a matter of religions, but history and culture.

135

You can already see how lousy this argument is. If Christianity is a religion, so is Islam. However, since Christianity is worldwide and Islam is still considered a religion of the Middle East, some schools permit the teaching of Islam. (We should also ask: how in the world are you going to teach about history in Western Europe—like the Reformation—without mentioning Christianity?!) In a way, it's a backhanded compliment to Christianity. Just as Jesus declared, His Word has gone out to all nations (Matthew 28:18–20). But it's still a lousy argument that allows people to teach any religion but Christianity in public schools.

it's Almost Time for Q&A. But First, Here's the Really Tricky Part . . .

This whole interaction between church and state is going to be really interesting in your lifetime, not to mention really tricky. On the one hand, you have secularism which wants to keep religion out of public life. On the other, you have multiculturalism which wants all religions—except Christianity—in public life. As always, it's going to be tough for Christians, since the world always welcomes any god except the one true God.

Here's the really, really tricky part for you. You're going to be pressured by secularism to deny your faith. But when you oppose secularism, you might find yourself helping multiculturalism. At other times, you're going to be pressured by multiculturalism to deny there's only one true Savior; but when you oppose this, you might find yourself helping secularism. That's why you want to make decisions very carefully; and even when you do, you won't always have a good feeling about them. This is why you give thanks that this world is not your final destination.

You're just passing through, because the one true Son of God went to the cross to give you eternal life in heaven.

Now, I could say a few more things, but you're already thinking them and you're about to start asking them in the questions. In what I've written up to now, you have all the information you need to solve them, so let's get to the Q&A.

Q & A:
You Ask . . .

138

75. is the United States federal government completely separated from religion?

No, and there are numerous examples. The United States Senate still pays for a chaplain to offer prayers at the start of sessions, while the U.S. Military retains chaplains for troops. Thanksgiving remains a federal holiday. Money still bears the phrase "In God We Trust," and the Supreme Court still begins proceedings with "God save the United States and this Honorable Court." As recently as June, 2004, the Supreme Court ruled that "under God" would remain in the Pledge of Allegiance. Belief in the existence of God, or at least a "Supreme Being," was foundational to the formation of the United States. Honestly, I don't think you'd have anything remotely like the current federal government if you removed all references to religion.

76. So is America a Christian nation?

It's sometimes said America is, or at least used to be, a "Christian nation," but I'm not sure what this means. Let's start with this: what makes you a Christian? You're a Christian because Jesus died on the cross for you. You're a Christian because He gave you forgiveness in Baptism and His Word, and still gives you more grace by His Word and Supper. In other words, you're a Christian by means of the Gospel.

Usually, when I hear people say that America began as a Christian nation, they go on to say the United States was built upon the "Judeo-Christian ethic." This means it was built on the ethics that Jews and Christians have in common. What do they have in common? The Law—the commandments of God, not the Gospel. Now, I'm quite happy to agree many of the ideals and concepts found in the Constitution are

139

in agreement with much of God's Law, but I don't find the Gospel in there anywhere. So while the formation of the United States reflects parts of God's Law, I wouldn't call it Christian because it doesn't proclaim Christ.

I'll also say, the more a nation's laws agree with God's Law, the better the nation is going to be. It will preach virtues like protection of the weak and unborn, service to one's neighbor, and the importance of good citizenship. But you don't turn people into Christians by passing laws; you curb crime and identify sin, but you don't give faith. Faith comes by the Gospel (Romans 1:16).

Others say America began as a Christian nation because, back in the "good old days," nearly everybody in America claimed to be Christian. However, remember the early settlers came from Europe, where your ruler's faith determined whether you were a Lutheran, an Anglican, or a Catholic. Thus, people claimed to be Christian because they were from a certain country, not because they were regular churchgoers. (For instance, 87% of people in Sweden today claim to be Lutheran, but only about 4% attend regular worship on a Sunday. Is Sweden really a Lutheran nation? I think not!) Only a small minority of early Americans attended worship regularly.

77. Even though secularism doesn't acknowledge God, isn't it really a religion?

Yes! Secularism is a religious (not scientific!) belief there is no God; therefore, it's up to man to decide right and wrong. Who says so? Among others, the United States Supreme Court declared "secular humanism" to be a religion in a case called *Torcaso vs. Watkins*. The Court notes it is one of many religions, like Buddhism and Taoism, which don't believe in a deity.

78. Should Christians be involved in politics?

Different people will give you different answers, so let me begin with this.

First off, remember the discussion we had earlier about the four ways that church and state can interact. Since a Christian isn't to isolate himself from the world, he's going to have to interact with government.

When it comes to politics, here's what makes Christians uncomfortable. God demands holiness in His Law. As Christians, then, we understand He doesn't tolerate compromise when it comes to keeping His commandments. He doesn't say, "Thou shalt not steal, except for the following reasons." We know, before God, compromise is not acceptable.

On the other hand, politics is all about compromise. In order to pass a law, politicians have to make the law appealing enough so that it gets enough votes to pass. This means most laws are going to be watered down from the original idea. Good legislation often has a lot of junk attached to it.

So if you're a Christian and a lawmaker, you're going to have some conflicts along the way. For instance, let's say a certain senator introduces a law to decrease the number of teen pregnancies in his state. It's based upon solid research and encourages abstinence. Similar laws have shown great results in other places. The law works. Unfortunately, the senator finds out he'll only get 48% of the vote, so it's going to fail. After discussions, another senator offers a compromise. He and some colleagues will vote for the bill if the law will help pay for "morning-after" pills for teenage girls. These pills are designed to cause an abortion after a baby has been conceived. If this is added to the bill, it's going to pass.

Now, you be the senator. If you accept the compromise, then the bill will pass and the number of teen pregnancies will decrease. However, it will also help pay for the killing of the unborn. If you reject the compromise, then the bill will fail and the number of teen pregnancies will continue to increase; this will likely lead to an overall increase in abortions. It's not an easy decision. What are you going to do?

Some will say, "I can't sponsor a bill including money for 'morning-after' pills, so I'm not going to compromise. I'll let the bill fail." To this senator, I would say, "It is good you follow your conscience. It's even better your salvation doesn't depend on how you vote, but on the truth that Jesus died and rose for you. Confess your sins—the ones you know about and the ones you don't, and rejoice to be forgiven."

Others will say, "I don't like the compromise, but

you ask about . . . LiFE

the outcome will decrease teen pregnancies and the overall number of abortions. Therefore, I'm willing to compromise." To this senator, I would say, "It is good you follow your conscience. It's even better your salvation doesn't depend on how you vote, but on the truth that Jesus died and rose for you. Confess your sins—the ones you know about and the ones you don't, and rejoice to be forgiven."

See what I mean? Because politics is all about compromise, you're not going to see many perfect laws get passed. A Christian politician must work for the best, understand he's not always going to get it, hold his nose sometimes and trust in His Savior.

Now, back to the question: should Christians be involved in politics?

These days, many non-Christians say, "No. Christians should not be involved in politics because their faith influences their opinions, and mixes church and state." Use your common sense on this argument. My first reaction is, "Well, duh. I sure hope a Christian's faith influences his opinions and life. Otherwise, it's not much of a faith." There's more, though, remember secularism is a religion, too. It is absolutely true a Christian's faith will influence his opinions and voting. It is also absolutely true that a secularist's lack of faith will do the same. Why is a godless voter better qualified to vote than a godly voter? This is one more example of how religion and government can't be totally separated.

You may also find Christians who say, "No. Christians should not be involved in politics because they must compromise their beliefs." Again, use common sense. Would it really be better if all Christians stopped running for office, stopped voting, and stopped writing to their congressmen? Would it really be better if only unbelievers were making laws? Do you think those laws would reflect God's Law much, and help preserve peace for the sake of the Gospel?

You'll find this to be true during elections, too. Some will argue, as a Christian, you can't vote for a candidate unless he's squeaky clean. Good luck finding a candidate who has never had to compromise. When it comes to politics, you'll have to vote for the best candidate, warts and all. This sometimes means holding your nose with one hand while you vote with the other. It may even mean you vote for a competent non-Christian instead of an incompetent believer.

So, yes: as citizens called upon by God to support their rulers, Christians should be involved in politics—whether that be running for office or just being a conscientious voter. They should understand not every law will be to their liking; and they should understand their salvation rests not on their success in lawmaking, but on Jesus their Savior.

79. Should there be prayer in public schools?

It's hard to believe, but it used to be common for public schools to begin the day with prayer (often the Lord's Prayer) and a reading from the Bible. After the Everson case, the lawsuits began. In 1962–63, three different cases made it to the Supreme Court using the Everson argument:

1. The Federal Government can't favor a particular religion or its prayers.

2. Therefore, state and local governments can't, either.

3. According to Everson, religion has no proper place in public schools.

4. Therefore state-sponsored prayers in public schools are unconstitutional.

5. Neener, neener, neener.

Each of the three cases sought to prohibit prayers which were sponsored by the schools, and each case succeeded. (If you're looking for a place to start, the most famous case was Murray vs. Curlett.) Local school boards, said the courts, had no right to require teachers to lead a class in prayer, even if the prayer was completely optional for the students.

Many individuals have campaigned for a return of prayer to public schools, maintaining it's a part of American heritage and arguing it will make the United States a more Christian nation. The argument for the return to school prayer often goes something like this: the original intent of the First Amendment was not to erase religion from public life, but to make sure all could exercise religion freely. The Everson decision went too far; and when a teacher offers a prayer it is completely optional for students, hardly infringing upon the rights of anyone. The return of school prayer, it's said, is simply a return to the First Amendment. To be perfectly honest, this is also an attempt to fight against secularism in the public schools.

It's not a bad argument. You might even hear someone argue it's the position Christians should take. But before you jump on the bandwagon, be careful! Remember what we said earlier: whenever you fight secularism, there's a good chance you'll be helping multiculturalism. The First Amendment says the government may not show favoritism to one religion over another: therefore, if public schools begin the day with prayer, they can't just have Christian prayers. If there's going to be prayer in public schools, you have one of two options.

First, you can have a prayer that's so meaningless it doesn't discriminate against anyone: "O god/goddess or whoever or whatever you might be (if you do indeed exist), please help us today by your gracious hand/tentacle/miscellaneous protrusion in ways we see fit and which would offend none here, all to the glory of no one in particular. Amen." A Christian simply can't join in praying this prayer, because it suggests all gods are equal.

Second, you can rotate prayers so each different religion is represented. You have a Christian prayer on Monday, then the Buddhist prayer on Tuesday, the Muslim prayer on Wednesday, and so forth. Once you get through all the religions represented in school, then you have a Christian prayer again. Now, do you really want a few weeks of prayers to false gods so you can hear one half-decent prayer? Once again, the rotation suggests religious differences don't matter, and all gods are pretty much the same as the one true God.

That's why I'm not big on fighting to restore prayer in public schools. Sure, it pokes secularism in the eye, but it really advances multiculturalism. It would never be a decent prayer. I'd advise you to keep prayer a personal thing in the classroom. Remember—as long as there are quizzes and tests, there will always be prayer in public schools anyway.

80. Did any of those court cases in the last question really include the phrase, "Neener, neener, neener"?

147

No, nor should they have.

81. Should there be religious monuments in public places, like buildings or parks?

Should there be a Christmas tree at city hall? Can there be a nativity scene in a public park? How about a monument of the Ten Commandments? Or a cross on publicly-owned land overlooking a town? May a county employee say "Merry Christmas," or only

"Happy Holidays?"

Unlike school prayer, which has been decided by the United States Supreme Court, debates over these issues are usually carried out at the local level. Once again, be really careful. Think this through before you speak.

Take, for instance, a city park having a monument of the Ten Commandments. One day, an atheist complains that this is a religious symbol on public property and asks it be removed. Others respond by saying the Ten Commandments are part of the heritage of the community, and they're not going to take down the monument because one guy doesn't like it. What would you argue? Before you answer, consider the following.

I live in Boise, Idaho, where an interesting variation on this story took place. A local city park had an old Ten Commandments monument few people even noticed. One day, a man from out of state arrived and announced he wanted to place another monument next to that one. His was a monument to hatred, a blasphemous statue; but it did have a Bible verse on the plaque. Before the city council, he argued they couldn't discriminate against him. If they were going to allow one religious statue, they would have to allow all religious statues.

Like school prayer, here are your choices: you can either have a park with no religious monuments, or allow every religion to place a monument its followers desire. You can either fight secularism and help multiculturalism, or vice versa. Whichever choice you make isn't going to leave you completely satisfied.

As for me, I'd prefer a park without a bunch of monuments. That way, the creation can simply declare its praise of the Lord (Psalm 148). Besides there's less stuff to run into while playing Frisbee.

82. i've heard of schools where students can display a Jewish Star of David or a Muslim Star and Crescent symbol, but not a cross. is that true?

It is true, for instance, in New York. The Star of David and Star and Crescent are considered to be cultural symbols, not religious symbols. Therefore, you can display them. A cross, however, is considered an exclusively religious symbol, so you can't display it. Even if everybody, their dog, and most rock stars are wearing crosses as jewelry, it's still considered a Christian symbol. Multiculturalism sure makes sense, doesn't it? (Hint: no.)

83. Should government ever interfere with religion?

One of the great freedoms that we enjoy in America is the freedom to practice religion without government censorship or interference. However, there is a time and a place where government should interfere and stop religious practices.

Imagine for a moment that you live in a town where there's a small group of people who worship fire, a rather pagan thing to do. For their weekly "worship," they gather around a big fire pit on a Thursday evening and light a big bonfire. They sit in a circle and sing songs about how cool fire is—or how hot—whatever. If this is their religion, they have every right to practice it in the United States of America. This is obviously a false religion that condemns them, but in America they have the right to be wrong.

However, imagine that, once a year, this group celebrates "Inferno," a grand fire festival where a bonfire just won't do. Instead, they march into town with torches, select a nice wooden house, and burn it to the ground as part of their worship for the night. The house doesn't belong to any of them, but to a citizen who doesn't worship fire.

Do you see what happens? A bonfire is a bonfire, and that's okay. Burning down someone's house is arson, which normally earns serious prison time. So, should the sheriff step in and arrest them for arson, or should he defend them because they were simply practicing their religious beliefs? In my opinion, lock 'em up!

Now religious arson is a pretty ridiculous example that hasn't happened, at least not to my knowledge. However, there are a lot of cases where government has intervened in a so-called religious practice. For instance, drug users claim their use of, say, LSD (a nasty illegal drug that makes you hallucinate) is their form of worshiping God, therefore they shouldn't be arrested for possession of illegal drugs. Others pay $25 for a certificate which says they're pastors. They then claim their home is a church, so they don't have to pay taxes on anything. In these cases, the government prosecutes drug users and tax evaders. It just goes to show some people will try anything to break the law and get away with it. Religion makes a nice cover for evildoing.

So far, the government usually only intervenes in religion when the religion's practices were hurting others, or when it was clear people were just using religion as an excuse. There is clearly a time when the state should step in and call a halt to religious practices. But where should we draw the line? For instance, imagine that someone leaves worship after Holy Communion and is involved in a fatal traffic accident. Is it possible that laws could be passed so Christians were no longer allowed to use wine at the Lord's Supper? It's not possible . . . yet. But who knows what could happen in the future?

84. if a church worker commits a crime, who should punish him: church officials or the state legal system?

This may sound like a no-brainer, but the subject has generated a lot of discussion recently, particularly because of publicity regarding the sexual abuse of children by clergy. From time to time, you'll also hear on the news about a group protesting the execution of a death row inmate because he's converted to Christianity.

Let's use some common sense first along with an example. Say a student gets caught cheating on a test by texting the answers on his cell phone to a buddy across the room. The principal suspends him for a couple of days and sends him home . . . where his parents are waiting. Which one of the following will probably happen?

> a. His parents will also punish him at home, because he disobeyed them and cheated at school.

> b. His parents will say, "We'd punish you, but since the crime happened at school, we really don't have any authority."

152

If his parents are halfway decent at raising kids, you can bet they're going to go for option "a." The student broke school rules, so the school punishes him; and since he broke family rules, the parents will discipline him, also.

The same principle applies to the question above. Remember, Christians are citizens of two kingdoms. If they violated God's Word and sin, then they are to be called to repentance by the Church (Matthew 18:15–18). If they broke the law of the state, then they are to be prosecuted by the state (Romans 13:2). If they broke the laws of both with one action, like murder, then they'll face discipline from both church and state. They don't get to pick one or the other.

So in the case of a priest or pastor who abuses

children, a church body has no right to hide the crime from authorities. Instead, the Church should stick to its mission of calling the man to repentance and absolving him if he repents, while cooperating with state authorities. While absolution removes the man's sin before God, it doesn't give him "get out of jail free" card from civil punishment. The state should stick to its mission of prosecuting a sexual predator in order to protect the innocent and keep order in society.

Or consider the example of the murderer scheduled for execution, but claims to convert to Christianity. It could be he's honestly confessed his sins and trusts in Christ; it could be he's faking it to get sympathy. Either way, he has still committed a crime, and the state still has the right to take his life. When he dies, however, he does so as one with the hope of eternal life in Christ.

153

85. How could a church ever argue it can prevent the state from prosecuting clergy for crimes?

The idea may seem baffling to you, especially if you've grown up as a Lutheran with the understanding that you're a citizen of both kingdoms. However, some church bodies believe, although not recognized by current governments, the Church still has authority over the state. When you hear someone arguing a church body has the right to shield its clergy, I'll bet you a nickel that he's from a denomination that believes the Church is in charge of the secular world.

86. is there ever a time when Christians should disobey the state?

Yes, and we have help here from Acts 5. Peter and the apostles are at the temple in Jerusalem, preaching about Jesus and performing miracles. They're arrested and brought before the Sanhedrin, the council that's in charge of both religious and civil life for the Jews. (The same group sentenced Jesus to death). The Sanhedrin is under the authority of the Roman Empire, but they still have a lot of power and firmly believe their doctrine should dictate civil life. The Sanhedrin warns the apostles to stop their activities and throws them in jail. That night, however, an angel releases them from prison and tells them to go back to the temple. They're arrested and brought before the Sanhedrin. The high priest demands to know why the apostles disobeyed the council, and Peter responds, "We must obey God rather than men" (Acts 5:29).

There you go—Christians should submit to the state as long as they can do so without violating God's Word. Christians may—and must—disobey the state if the state commands them to disobey God's Word. At such times, Christians will likely suffer civil punishment, maybe prison or death, for doing so. In such dire times, however, the people of God remain faithful to the Lord. After all, it's the Lord who redeemed them from their sin to give them everlasting life. All will stand before the Lord on Judgment Day.

History is full of examples of Christians who died for their faith. A famous example is Polycarp, a Christian thrown to wild beasts because he refused to worship the false gods of the Roman Empire. Sometimes, it's clear-cut. Remember, though, life is messy, and it will not always be so clear. For instance, may a Christian pay his federal taxes with a clear conscience if some of the money is used to fund abortions? Most Christians in America apparently answer "yes" at this point, especially as long as the Church continues to work for the preservation of life. But how many sinful programs may a government sponsor before a Christian can't help finance it anymore? That's a difficult question, because Christians draw the line at different spots along the way.

155

87. You've expressed a lot of concerns in this section. Does this mean you don't like America very much?

Not at all! The freedoms you and I enjoy in this country are amazing and unheard of in history. Christians have lived in nations that threatened them with punishment, even death, if they were baptized, heard the Word, or received Holy Communion. Many Christians still live in such places today. You and I live in a nation that not only allows us to practice Christian worship, but defends our right to do so! This is a freedom that we largely take for granted; yet most Christians have never known such a privilege before.

You have incredible freedoms and rights as an

American citizen, too. You have the freedom to vote for candidates who seek to see the First Amendment interpreted correctly. You even have the freedom to be the candidate! You are free to write to your congressional representatives, even testify before congressional sub-committees. You have the protected freedom to make your voice heard. The United States is still a government of the people, by the people, for the people. If there was ever a time for Christians to be aware of the issues and to make their voice heard, the time is now. However, it is important to do it intelligently and responsibly.

Our nation has its share of problems and manifest sins, to be sure. But there's no place I'd rather be on this earth.

One of the problems we Americans have is we are historically shortsighted. This nation is less than 230 years old, barely out of diapers compared to others. However, we tend to believe our nation is the norm in history. It seems most Americans are under the impression people throughout history have freely elected their rulers, freely practiced their religion, always enjoyed safety, and always had enough to eat. It simply isn't so. Prior to the United States, almost every nation was ruled by a king, often a tyrant, where the people had no vote or voice on laws and rulers. Often, nations were plagued by marauders and raiding armies—villages were wiped out. In fact, kingdoms were most stable when the laws were cruel. At the time of Jesus' birth and death, the Roman Empire was peaceful because the Romans terrified everybody to keep them from rebelling. Normally meat wasn't a part of daily the menu, but so precious it was reserved only for special occasions.

This isn't just true in past history, but in the present. Many nations today still have tyrants where citizens have no rights, where food is scarce and disease is uncontrolled. If you don't believe me, take a trip to Sudan . . . or the Congo . . . or North Korea. Try handing out Bibles to people on the street in Iran.

(Each situation has its temptations for Christians. American Christians tend to be so prosperous and safe they don't take sin and death—and the need for forgiveness—seriously. Christians in a hostile place like Darfur, on the other hand, are tempted to despair and believe God has abandoned them.)

My point is this: America is not the norm in history. America, with its freedoms and prosperity, is an abnormality. The question remains: will democracy spread worldwide and set more people free, or will this experiment collapse back into tyranny? Given the current state of the world, it could go either way.

But based upon what Scripture says about the sinfulness of man, tyranny comes easier than freedom, often disguising slavery as liberation. And based upon history, every nation eventually comes to an end.

So here's where your ultimate hope lies: while you're a citizen of a nation in this world, you're really only passing through. Way back in the Old Testament, the Israelites spent a lot of time in the wilderness on the way to the Promised Land. For you, this world is the wilderness and the Promised Land is heaven. What is said of God's people of old is also said of you: "But as it is, they desire a better country, that is, a heavenly one. Therefore God is not ashamed to be called their God, for He has prepared for them a city" (Hebrews 11:16). How about that? Heaven is yours because—thanks to Jesus' death for sin, God is not ashamed of you.

One Final Answer One More Time

You made it to the last pages! I thank you for reading. I hope this book has been helpful.

At the beginning I told you there was an infinite number of questions out there, and an even greater number of answers. That's really bad math, but hey, I'm a pastor. Here's some more bad math—the infinite number of questions is growing more infinite. It's growing infiniter, if we want to add bad grammar to my list of errors. The reason is, with each new development, new questions arise. For instance, scientists come up with new medical procedures all the time. Each time, the questions must be asked: Is it ethical? Is it good? How can it be used? How might it be abused? Who will make that decision? It's true—not just with medicine, but computers, video games, clothes, activities, and more.

I'm tired of questions, because they keep on coming. But being tired is no excuse to stop answering them, because this is part of the Christian's life in this world. I'll tell you this, though: part of my sanity each day comes with this unshakeable truth: no matter the mysteries and problems of life in this world, there's no question about eternal life. No matter the aggravating dilemmas of this world we're just passing through. Heaven is a sure thing, because it's already been answered. When Jesus died on the cross, eternal life was won. When you were baptized, He gave it personally to you. Throughout your life, He keeps giving you grace and life in His Word and His Holy Supper. You and I aren't going to know all the answers of this world; even when we do, we're going to make some really bad decisions. So once again, rejoice in this—eternal life doesn't depend on how well you answer questions. Confess yours sins, rejoice in Jesus' forgiveness, and give thanks for this final answer:

> For all the promises of God find their
> Yes in Him [in Jesus!]. That is why it is
> through Him that we utter our Amen
> to God for His glory.
> **(2 Corinthians 1:20)**

Indeed, Jesus is the unfailing answer who gives eternal life . . . this is most certainly true.

So we utter our "Amen" to God.